ACHIEVING PEAK PERFORMANCE

A STEP BY STEP SYSTEM TO GROW A
WELL TRAINED, EDUCATED, AND MOTIVATED
TEAM FOR THE 21ST CENTURY

NIDO R. QUBEIN

BEST SELLERS
PUBLISHING

Minneapolis, Minnesota, USA

Creative Services, Inc.
806 Westchester Drive, P. O. Box 6008
High Point, North Carolina 27262 USA
Telephone 910-889-3010
Facsimile 910-885-3001

For quantity purchases of this book contact:

Best Sellers Publishing
9201 East Bloomington Freeway
Minneapolis, Minnesota 55420 USA
Telephone 612-888-7672
Facsimile 612-884-8901

Publisher's Cataloging in Publication

Qubein, Nido R.
    Achieving peak performance: a step by step system to grow a well trained, educated and motivated team for the 21st century / by Nido R. Qubein
    p.   cm.
    Includes bibliographical references.
    ISBN 0-9636268-5-X

    1. Training.   2. Education.   I. Title.

658.312   95-083691

Printed in Colombia

Also by Nido Qubein

Stairway to Success

How to Be a Great Communicator

Get the Best From Yourself

Communicate Like a Pro

Nido Qubein's Techniques
of Professional Selling

What Works and What
Doesn't Work in Youth Work

Selling Savvy

Positioning Power

Marketing Professional Services

The Crestcom Management Series

To Deena,
With love.

Acknowledgments

This book is the result of my first-hand experience with clients in the United States and around the world. The ideas and strategies I share with you here would be theoretical at best if it weren't for the creative and innovative corporate executives who believed in me and engaged me as their consultant. They provided me the platform to enhance and improve my concepts for growing more productive, better educated employees.

I specifically wish to thank INA Bearing Company and its chief executive, Bruce Warmbold, for entrusting me with their sales and management teams since 1978. It has been a most fulfilling relationship to serve this world-class needle bearing manufacturer.

Few business leaders enjoy Paula Marshall Chapman's hunger for constantly building better quality products and her thirst for delivering outstanding customer service. How privileged I am to have served Paula's company, Bama Foods, since 1986.

To Southern National Corporation and its subsidiary, BB&T Bank, I owe heartfelt gratitude for the opportunity to help in educating their 10,000 plus employees serving customers in hundreds of cities. Chairman and CEO John Allison IV is uncompromising when it comes to providing the best learning systems for his people. And so is the rest of the executive team.

In the international arena, I've thoroughly enjoyed my involvement with Ken Pitman's Euronet, based in Luxembourg and serving ten European countries. Ken translated my books in German and Dutch and offered me memorable opportunities few consultants ever experience.

Graeme Clegg, Chairman of New Image International in New Zealand, invited our help in his home country as well as in Australia, Singapore, Malaysia and Indonesia — and became a dear personal friend, too.

How fortunate I've been to receive warm hospitality from so many special clients; but none surpass André Herman's touch for first class treatment. Our work with André's company, TDC Bull, in Brazil has been a splendid treasure.

For the last two decades I've served as consultant to great companies: Dole, Radio Shack, U.S. Furniture Industries, Industrial Housekeeping, Sebastian, W & J Rives, PIC, New Home Specialist, Floyd Wickman Companies, Carlson Learning, Concord Telephone, American Airlines, and dozens more. How blessed I am to have been associated with such progressive organizations.

The research, writing, and editing of this book and others I've offered would have never been completed without the wise guidance and proven abilities of Gene Owens and Tom Watson.

Thank you all.

CONTENTS

CHAPTER ONE

YOU NEED MORE THAN A TRAINING DEPARTMENT

If your organization has only a training department, it's simply not enough.

To paraphrase Stanley Marcus, you don't train people. You train dogs and seals and elephants. People you *educate*.

You may find that opening statement radical and unsettling. And you might expect your training director to respond with boos, hisses and rock-throwing.

But when I say "Replace your training department with a *Department of Education and Development*," the clattering sound you hear is not from rocks being thrown at me by training directors and human-resource people across the land. It's applause — applause from the very people you might expect to do the rock throwing. They're applauding because they know I'm right. And furthermore, I'm saying what the best of them have been saying with increasing urgency.

Let me be clear: I'm not saying that training is unnecessary. I have the utmost respect for the gifted and talented people who help people learn the ropes of their jobs. They play an important and necessary role in the success of any organization.

But the people most deeply involved in grooming corporate work forces for success know that it isn't enough to teach people the step-by-step on-the-job process. Something more is needed. Knowledge-able human-resource people will tell you that:

- Technical training *alone* does not result in better productivity or better quality. To achieve peak performance, employees must be properly motivated.

- You can't motivate people; they act on their own motives, not yours. But education will help them understand how their best interests parallel the best interests of the organization. Then they will be *self*-motivated to help the organization achieve its goals.

- Education is broad, affecting the whole person. Training is often narrow, imparting technical skill without necessarily influencing behavior. Education builds in self-confidence, self-esteem, initiative, and human understanding in ways that transform the individual.

- Education enhances productivity. Education can foster an atmosphere in which people cooperate with rather than competing with others in the organization. When people within an organization compete, there's likely to be a hoarding of ideas and information. When people cooperate, these ideas are shared, to the benefit of the entire organization.

- Education enhances quality. Education instills attitudes that value excellence. Training can impart the skills necessary to achieve excellence, but without the proper attitude, no amount of training will assure quality.

- Education, coupled with a good training system, enhances external competitiveness. An organization that knows what it is and where it is going is in excellent position to serve its customers well and to get the jump on the competition.

LEADING VS. DRAGGING

Let us define what we mean by *training* and *education*. Training deals with *external* skills. Education deals with what a person is on the *inside*. Both are necessary to the modern organization. Many executives, though, assume that once their employees know *how* to do their jobs, the company is ready to speed smoothly down the freeway of excellence. They overlook the importance of *why*. Education supplies the *why*, thus giving employees a reason to get onto the freeway in the first place.

The word *education* comes from the Latin *ducere*, which means *to lead*.

The word *training* comes from the Latin *trahere*, which means *to drag* or *to draw*.

If you're training your employees without educating them, you're dragging them toward your goals.

If you're educating them, you're leading them toward your goals. When you lead people, you induce them to follow you of their own free will and in their own self-interest. When that happens, you and they join in a common effort to achieve excellence. With good technical *training* enhanced by a well-rounded *education*, your organization will have what it takes to survive and thrive in the new, fast-paced, quality-demanding marketplace.

Why do I say that education leads to excellence while training *alone* can drag you into mediocrity?

TEN MAJOR DIFFERENCES

Let's get beyond dictionary definitions and talk about ten distinctions between training and education in the work place. Effective training directors, of course, understand these points and are committed to achieving solid results which impact their organizations positively.

DISTINCTION NO. 1:
TRAINING TEACHES PEOPLE WHAT TO *DO*.
EDUCATION TEACHES PEOPLE WHAT TO *BE*.

Is the person who answers your telephone a telephone receptionist or a member of your corporate team?

The receptionist knows what to do: answer on the proper ring, give the standard greeting, and push the right buttons to connect the caller with the proper party.

So you're in a conference with your sales staff when a customer calls with a big order.

"Your party will be with you in a moment; I'll put you on hold," says the receptionist.

So the right buttons are punched in the right sequence, and your customer is entertained with soft music while you continue with your conference. The receptionist's job has been done.

Ten minutes later, you're still in the conference, and the customer has hung up and placed the order with a competitor.

The receptionist has been *trained* to operate the telephone system, but not *educated* to be a member of your corporate team. Education would emphasize that every member of the team is involved in customer service whenever and wherever there is contact with a customer. So the receptionist would be taught to *be* someone — an important team member — and not to *do* something — answer the telephone.

There's nothing wrong with teaching a person what to do. If a person's job is to open Valve A, throw Lever B and push Button C in that sequence, it's essential that the employee learn to do that. That's training.

But suppose the person who runs the machine becomes part of a self-managed team. That team may be charged with maintaining equipment, managing inventory, benchmarking for quality, and monitoring input and output. Suppose you're operating on the

Economic Value-Added (EVA) premise, and each function is expected to show that the value added exceeds the real cost of capital utilized. The employee who has only been trained but not educated is going to say "Huh?" That's because training teaches people to *do* specific tasks, without relating them to the overall mission of the company. Successful companies have found that technical training, to be of any maximum value, must be part of comprehensive education and development.

DISTINCTION NO. 2:
TRAINING IS ANCHORED TO THE PAST.
EDUCATION LOOKS TOWARD THE FUTURE.

Training teaches people to perform repetitive tasks the same way, over and over. The methods are based on time-tested procedures. But these days, procedures change rapidly. During the 1950s, IBM could produce the same product for nine years before it became obsolete. By 1988, the cycle had shrunk to less than 18 months for many product lines, and as little as six months for some.[1] Technology changes so fast that 20% of an engineer's knowledge becomes obsolete every year. In such an environment, it's not enough that people have a one-time learning experience. They must acquire attitudes that dispose them toward *constant* learning; that keep them constantly looking for new things to learn.

DISTINCTION NO. 3:
WHEN CIRCUMSTANCES CHANGE,
TRAINING HAS TO BE UNLEARNED.
EDUCATION CAN BE BUILT UPON.

When you train people for specific tasks and the tasks become obsolete — as they inevitably will —

then the training becomes a dead-end. All the habits and procedures that have been drilled into the worker must now be undrilled, and a new set of habits and procedures substituted.

But if a worker has been educated in innovative thinking and behavior, the knowledge remains and the worker can build on it as the company changes — and can help the company to make the changes necessary to meet future challenges.

Alvin Toffler wrote about the sad results of dead-end training when he described a visit to a foundry in Ontario much like the one he once worked in:

> *The thing that struck me was not just that those workers couldn't walk across the street and get jobs in Silicon Valley, but that the managers couldn't either. Their style of management was wrong. Their culture was wrong. Their lifestyle was wrong. The way they spoke was wrong. The way they dressed was wrong — everything was wrong. They were highly successful at what they had been trained to do. But . . . along came a new culture.*[2]

DISTINCTION NO. 4:
TRAINING DEALS WITH ACTIONS. EDUCATION DEALS WITH THOUGHTS AND FEELINGS.

Education recognizes the fact that external actions are preceded by internal thoughts and feelings. We *think*, we *feel*, and then we *act*.

Training ignores the *thoughts* and *feelings* and addresses only the *actions*. The company that invests only in training may end up with workers who know *how* to do the job but don't understand *why* they should do it, and thus lack the motivation to do it properly.

I'm reminded of the football coach who trained a talented player named Charlie as a running back. He taught him all the skills and all the moves. In the key game against a huge, aggressive defense, the coach told the quarterback, "Give the ball to Charlie."

On the first play, the quarterback faked a handoff to Charlie, but kept the ball — and was clobbered by the defensive line.

"Give the ball to Charlie," yelled the coach.

Again and again, the quarterback faked the handoff, kept the ball and was creamed.

On fourth down and 20, the coach finally called his quarterback to the sidelines.

"I thought I told you to give the ball to Charlie," he said.

"I know, Coach," replied the quarterback, "but Charlie says he don't *want* the ball."

If you ignore thoughts and feelings and concentrate solely on actions, you'll end up with a work force full of Charlies who have the abilities but don't want to carry the ball. All the skills they acquired through training will go for naught.

Education influences actions by first addressing thoughts and feelings. It produces a team full of highly motivated Charlies.

DISTINCTION NO. 5:
TRAINING TEACHES *HOW.*
EDUCATION TEACHES *WHY.*

Would you want your teen-ager to have sex education or sex training? Sex training can teach teen-agers *how* to have sex. But it can't teach the deeper meanings involved in personal relationships. It can't teach love and mutual trust. It can't teach responsibility. It can't teach respect for oneself and one's partner. These are inner qualities that come from education.

Similarly, you can't *train* employees to understand the deeper meaning of their job tasks; to relate them to the overall mission of the company. Training a person to operate a machine or follow a procedure doesn't instill a passion for quality. It doesn't inspire loyalty to the company. It doesn't impart team spirit and doesn't endow the recipient with the ability to work smoothly and cooperatively with co-workers.

David A. Garvin, professor of business administration at the Harvard Business School, seems to agree with what I've been telling my clients. He wrote:

> *Most training programs focus primarily on problem-solving techniques, using exercises and practical examples. These tools are relatively straightforward and easily communicated; the necessary mind-set, however, is more difficult to establish. Accuracy and precision are essential for learning. Employees must therefore become more disciplined in their thinking and more attentive to details. They must continually ask, "How do we know that's true?" recognizing that close enough is not good enough if real learning is to take place. They*

must push beyond obvious symptoms to assess underlying causes, often collecting evidence when conventional wisdom says it is unnecessary. Otherwise, the organization will remain a prisoner of "gut facts" and sloppy reasoning, and learning will be stifled.[3]

DISTINCTION NO. 6:
TRAINING CAN GIVE PEOPLE COMPETENCE. EDUCATION ENABLES THEM TO PUT THEIR COMPETENCE TO GOOD USE FOR THE COMPANY.

It may surprise you to know that technical competence is not the principal mark of the successful person, even in high-tech jobs.

A study of computer programmers at Bell Laboratories showed that the star performers outperformed moderate performers by a margin of 8-1. Yet, there was little meaningful difference between the innate abilities of the stars and those of the mediocrities. You don't get through the door at Bell Laboratories unless you're very smart. The real distinction was found in the top performers' approaches to their jobs.

These approaches did not involve mechanical processes. They involved such things as taking initiative and networking with other individuals in the organization. The difference between mediocrity and excellence lay in inner qualities and not external skills.

DISTINCTION NO. 7:
TRAINING FOCUSES ON PROCEDURES.
EDUCATION FOCUSES ON PEOPLE.

Education puts the emphasis where it belongs: on a company's most valuable asset. That asset is not buildings, equipment, inventory or brand equity. It is the commitment, energy and ingenuity of its people. These qualities can turn ordinary people into an extraordinary work force. An extraordinary person is someone who consistently does the things ordinary people can't do or won't do. So if you want your ordinary people to become extraordinary people, you simply need to give them strong reasons to do the things ordinary people *won't* do and teach them to do the things ordinary people *can't* do.

We are living in an era of rapid change, and a company's success depends upon its ability to change. These changes cannot be effected simply by changing rules and policies. To manage change successfully, you must be able to change the way people think and feel. These new thoughts and feelings will lead to new behaviors. You change thoughts and feelings through education.

DISTINCTION NO. 8:
TRAINING FOCUSES ON THE INDIVIDUAL.
EDUCATION FOCUSES ON THE
ORGANIZATION.

No one individual can acquire all the knowledge and skills needed to make an organization successful. The knowledge and skills must be held collectively by the entire work force, but they must be shared among the individuals in the work force. The organization must be able to talk to itself: Its people must be taught to communicate with one another across functional and departmental lines and up and down the corporate ladder. If you train one individual to execute one procedure properly, that individual may be useless for any other task required. Furthermore, the individual's skills won't improve the performance of any other individual within the work force, unless the individual finds some way to share them or to apply them in ways that complement the skills of others.

The ability to communicate effectively across functional and supervisory lines is one of the most crucial abilities in the modern organization. The organization's people must acquire that ability through education. It can't be produced through training.

DISTINCTION NO. 9: TRAINING TEACHES PEOPLE TO FOLLOW PRESCRIPTIONS. EDUCATION TEACHES PEOPLE TO MAKE CHOICES.

We can't grow by repeatedly following prescriptions. We can grow only by making new choices. We are the sum total of the choices we have made in the past. We can change what we are in the future through the choices we make today.

Paul Allaire, as CEO of Xerox, led his company — in a stunning comeback — to preeminence in the field of document copiers. Allaire observed that "to do things differently, we must learn to see things differently."

Throughout my two decades as a management consultant, I've seen Allaire's observation repeatedly borne out, and I've reached one further conclusion: We can't see things differently through a formulaic approach that overlooks inner behavior.

Don't just take my word for it. People who work on the leading edge of change agree with me. For instance, John Seely Brown, chief scientist and director of Xerox's Palo Alto Research Center, wrote:

> *In physics, folklore has it that the current generation of physicists must pass away before the field can adopt a new way to "see" the world. In the business world, we can't wait that long. We must find ways — nitty-gritty ways — to continually grind new conceptual lenses, and. . . direct or formulaic approaches won't work[4] (emphasis mine).*

DISTINCTION NO. 10:
TRAINING IS A PROGRAM.
EDUCATION IS A PROCESS.

A program has a beginning and an end. A process is a continuing thing. Once a trainee has mastered a technique, training has accomplished its purpose.

Within a few weeks, you can teach clerical workers all they need to know about operating the copying machine, sending a fax, and entering and retrieving data through a computer. You can teach production workers all they need to know about assembling a product. But if that's all you teach them, you are severely limiting their growth opportunities. They can become only so good at these mechanical tasks.

Education, in contrast, offers a much broader, long-term approach that places no limit on human growth. To bring out the full potential of your people, you need to think beyond the immediate task, beyond the department or function in which it is performed, and even beyond the organization. Human development is bigger than training — bigger than any seminar or course.

As a corporate executive, you are rightly concerned with your return on investment — your ROI — and your return on equity — your ROE.

To achieve healthy ROI and ROE, you must help your employees achieve their *own* ROE — return on effort — and a healthy ROL — return on life. Employees who have learned to seek and master challenges, and employees who find that their jobs enrich their lives, will happily exert themselves to enrich the company's bottom line.

A work force educated to embrace challenge will look for and embrace new and better techniques. A good educational process is the best guarantee of constant improvement.

IT TAKES EDUCATION TO PRODUCE LEADERS

Education and development are not just for the people in the ranks of an organization. Executive development requires education. Narrowly focused training programs alone do not produce good leaders. A talented executive who is trained to perform the duties of a controller may be lost when placed in an executive position that requires a broad knowledge of the company and its people. Education provides the broad knowledge needed to produce effective executives.

Corporations have no choice but to invest substantial resources in developing people. So it's best to invest in ways that let people grow; that teach them to think for themselves; that create a pool of solid candidates for promotion to higher positions.

Training Alone
Cannot Produce a Vision

Teaching people skills without giving them a vision for a better future — a vision based on common values — is only training.

Training is anchored to the past, and as Charles Kettering said: "You can't have a better tomorrow if you're thinking about yesterday."

We've spent entirely too much time in the past teaching people what to do instead of concentrating on how they think and how they feel and how they behave; far too much time getting a job done instead of producing excellent results; far too much time conforming instead of creating.

Go Where the Puck
is Going to Be

Yesterday's thinking looks at the tasks people perform today and asks, "How can we train our future employees to do these things?"

Today's thinking looks at the kind of people needed to fulfill corporate strategy and finds ways to teach staff and employees to *become* that kind of people.

A reporter once asked Wayne Gretzky, the great hockey player, why he always seemed to be where the puck was. Gretzky replied, "I don't do that at all. I always go to where the puck is going to be."

Executives, too, must go where the action is going to be. They need to look down the road 5 or 10 years and ask "What kind of company do we want to be by then, and what kind of employees will it take to get us there?" Then they can plan educational and development programs to develop such employees.

To carry out such programs, you need behavioral change agents in addition to trainers. Behavioral facilitators nurture lasting qualities that won't become obsolete when the next technological breakthrough occurs.

MORE THAN SEMANTICS

You may be thinking that the distinction between training and education is just a matter of semantics. I've heard it said that training and education are identical because "learning is learning by doing."

But that's like saying that bananas and oranges are identical because you have to peel both before eating them.

Let's take a simple example: learning to drive a car. You can train youngsters to drive an automobile by letting them practice all the mechanical steps involved in starting it, stopping it and keeping it in the road.

But to teach them respect for traffic laws; to teach them to practice courtesy on the road; to teach them to maintain their vehicles in safe condition requires more than training; it requires the inculcating of inner attitudes that affect outward behavior. You can *train* people to drive automobiles. But you have to *educate* them to become safe, responsible drivers. Both the training and the education are necessary.

Similarly, you can train people to perform the routine tasks related to your business. But you must educate them to seek excellence. Most people would rather be comfortable than to be excellent. You change that attitude through consistent input that appeals to an individual's self-interest and organizational spirit.

My speaking invitations lately have come heavily from companies going through major restructuring, right-sizing and revamping. Employees are expected to understand, cooperate, embrace change and nurture teamwork. Training alone won't set the stage for these dramatic adjustments. Proper attitude is achieved from a constant educational process aimed at building a consistent desire for excellence.

So it isn't enough that you change the name of your training department to "Education and Development Department." To succeed in the global marketplace, you must help your employees to make the inner changes required to achieve and maintain competitiveness.

This is the theme I'm hearing from more and more people in human-resources departments, and from more and more students of human behavior in the work place. Your human-resources professionals want to educate the people, and they're appealing to management for the necessary tools.

You can help them develop your human component through an educational system that rests on seven conceptual pillars. In the next chapter we will identify those pillars, and in succeeding chapters we will examine them one by one.

CHAPTER TWO

THE SEVEN PILLARS OF WORK-PLACE EDUCATION

An effective educational system forms a solid foundation for business success in today's climate. A good educational system rests on seven conceptual pillars that will provide solid support for your organization's objectives. Here are the pillars I have identified after years of consulting with organizations, both profit and non-profit in the U.S. and abroad:

1. *Education for the whole individual.* A good educational system improves the whole individual — the mind as well as the reflexes.

2. *An integrated learning process.* A good corporate educational system educates the entire organization through an integrated approach.

3. *Education for partnership between management and employees.* Effective education eliminates

the adversarial relationship between management and employees, and guides them into a mutually beneficial partnership.

4. *Education for congruence.* Your educational process should enable your employees to form personal visions that are congruent with the corporate vision, creating a powerful synergy for individual and corporate success.

5. *Education for a quality-based culture.* An educational system should lead to a quality-oriented mental disposition. In the quest for excellence, thisis far more important than the learning of mechanical techniques.

6. *Education for The three P's:* A good educational process will enhance employee output in proportion to input, and thus promote the Three P's: performance, productivity and profitability. The Motorola Corporation estimates that each dollar it spends on educating its employees delivers $30 in productivity in 3 years. That's dramatic payback.

7. *Education to reinforce your differential advantage.* Education should help your employees identify and exploit your differential advantage and thus achieve maximum effectiveness in the marketplace.

YOU DON'T HAVE TO SEND THEM TO MIT OR HARVARD

Many people equate *education* with MBA's and *training* with skilled workers. Many businesses are sending personnel to technical and community colleges to further their development, and some educational institutions are inaugurating programs aimed at rounding out the business and leadership skills needed by today's executives.

But the human-resources professionals I encounter in my consulting work are convinced that educational programs designed only for the upper echelons are far too shallow. Every job that requires thinking, motivated people calls for an educational approach.

That doesn't mean you have to send your machine operators to MIT, or your customer-service representatives to Harvard Business School.

You can erect the seven pillars of corporate education under your own roof, using your own personnel. You do it by first deciding where you want to go with your company. Then you devise a plan for developing in your people the qualities and attitudes that will take you where you want to go. A skilled consultant can assess the educational needs of your work force and design a strategy for addressing those needs on a continuing basis.

In consulting with business executives on five continents over two decades, I've learned that all business organizations have three things in common:

1. A product.
2. A process.
3. A person.

The product may be tangible, such as an automobile, a piece of furniture or a refrigerator. Or it may be intangible, such as financial services, overnight hospitality or information.

The process may involve mechanical or chemical actions, or procedures for delivering services.

But it's the *person* who carries out the processes and produces the products.

Corporations invest huge sums in the buildings, tools and equipment necessary to the process. They also spend megabucks on designing, marketing and selling the product.

Why shouldn't they invest just as aggressively in the person?

"American companies," asserted Robert Reich, President Clinton's secretary of labor, "have got to be urged to treat their workers as assets to be developed rather than as costs to be cut."[1]

When you build a new building or buy a new piece of equipment, you budget the money to maintain it. When you hire new employees, do you budget money to educate and develop them? And do you invest in the first pillar — education of the whole person?

Money spent maintaining equipment is repaid and then some in the form of longer life, fewer breakdowns, lower operating costs, and higher productivity.

Money spent developing the work force is repaid through higher productivity, higher quality, greater innovation, and more competitiveness in the marketplace.

Dealing with problems in product and process without dealing with the human element is like dealing with a flat tire without dealing with air. The finest steel-belted radial is worthless without the air that inflates it. The finest physical plant and equipment are worthless without the people who keep them operating.

THE "SOFT STUFF" IS VITAL

Executives traditionally have made a distinction between "hard training" — the teaching of specific skills — and "soft training" — education aimed at influencing behavior through thoughts and feelings.

Increasingly, human-resources people are insisting that "hard" skills alone won't pave the road to success.

At Levi Strauss, Robert Haas became a believer. As chairman of the clothing company, he led it through a transition from traditional management to participative management. Contrasting the old culture with the new, he observed:

> *The soft stuff was the company's commitment to our work force. And the hard stuff was what really mattered: getting pants out the door. What we've learned is that the soft stuff and the hard stuff are becoming increasingly intertwined. A company's values — what it stands for, what its people believe in — are crucial to its competitive success. Indeed, values drive the business.*[2]

"Soft skills," such as communication, commitment, and cooperation, yield impressive results in the modern organization. The second educational pillar — an integrated learning process — will assure that these soft skills are spread throughout your organization.

THE CORPORATE OMELET

The old-style corporation was like a carton of eggs, each unit enclosed in an individual shell, separated by barriers that kept them from rubbing together. The modern corporation is like an omelet, the various units blending their talents and interests to produce a harmonious whole.

When interaction was kept to a minimum, the "soft skills" were not considered important.

Let's draw an analogy between the work place and the classroom. Picture a high-school classroom in which a teacher is administering an exam. Each student is expected to come up with the right solutions to the problems. In such a setting, some will succeed and some will fail, but few will solve all the problems. Those who do find the right answers won't share them with others. That would be cheating. In that kind of setting, who needs skills in communication and cooperation?

Suppose the teacher were to say, "I'm not testing you as individuals; I'm testing you as a class. Put your heads together and come up with the answers."

In such a situation, skills in communication and cooperation would suddenly become very important. In all likelihood, no individual would possess all the knowledge needed to solve the problems or all the aptitudes needed to apply the knowledge. But the class as a whole would have the knowledge and aptitudes. Communication and cooperation would spread the knowledge throughout the group, and the problems would be solved. Instead of some people succeeding and some failing, everyone would succeed.

What was traditionally known as cheating in the typical classroom is known as collaborative problem-solving in the work place. It is the key to success in today's business world. Where people are educated to share and compare instead of hoard and compete, they produce higher quality and achieve greater productivity.

GOING BEYOND TECHNICAL TRAINING

The learning that has propelled such organizations as Motorola, General Electric, Honeywell and Xerox to the front ranks of successful companies does not stop at technical training. Technical training is just one part of a broad, well-planned approach. Employees in these companies learn far more than the mechanics of their jobs.

They learn:

- Problem-solving.
- Problem prevention.
- Communication.
- Stress management.
- Time management.
- Strategic planning.
- Self evaluation.
- Change management.
- How to foster creativity.
- How to profit from their own experiences.
- How to profit from the experiences of others.

SOFT STUFF AND THE BOTTOM LINE

Ignoring the "soft stuff" can be devastating to the bottom line. Poor communication alone can take large bites out of your profits. It can result in employee anger, frustration and alienation. It can bring about wasted effort, low productivity and high turnover.

Suppose your company employs 500 people, and each of them makes one mistake per year as a result of faulty communication. If each mistake costs you only $100, it will reduce your profits by $50,000 — and you can bet that in actual experience the cost is much higher. If 100 million American workers were to commit one such mistake each year, the cost to business would be $10 billion.

SOFT SKILLS AND PARTICIPATIVE MANAGEMENT

The "soft stuff" is absolutely essential to participative management, the management style supported by the third pillar — partnership between employees and management.

Well-managed companies make sure that their executives, managers, and supervisors understand the human-relations principles necessary to make participative management work.

Konosuke Matsushita, head of Matsushita Electric Industrial Company Ltd., expressed it well when he said, "First, we must really know what a human being is. If one wants to raise sheep, one must first learn the nature of sheep. So with the human heart."[3]

Humans aren't sheep, and corporations don't "raise" their employees. But to get the most out of your work force, it's essential that your management and supervisory personnel know about human nature.

MERGING THE THREE MAINSTREAMS

Creating an educated organization entails a merging of three mainstreams of corporate emphasis that have marked the last three decades. In the 1970s, the emphasis was on motivation. In the 1980s, it was on training. In the 1990s, it has been on mobilization. Tomorrow's company must merge all these streams.

Management cannot motivate its employees. But it can create a motivational environment. Such an environment needs managers and supervisors who are educated in human-relations skills.

Management must provide training. The new generation of workers comes to the job with woefully inadequate skills. These newcomers not only lack the technical skills to perform the routine tasks they are called upon to perform; a dismaying proportion of them also lack the basic reading, writing and simple mathematics skills. These skills must be imparted, but they must be accompanied by an educational program aimed at instilling productive, quality-conscious attitudes.

THE NEW GENERATION
AND THE FOURTH PILLAR

The fourth pillar of a corporate educational system supports congruence between the corporate vision and the personal visions of individuals.

This pillar will assume even greater importance as the "Baby Boom" generation retires and the "Baby Bust" generation replaces it. The Baby Boomers represent the heavy crop of babies born between 1946 and 1964, in the aftermath of World War II and Korea. The Baby Busters represent the sparse generation resulting from the family planning that followed the introduction of the birth-control pill.

Authors Lawrence J. Bradford and Claire Raines tell us that members of the "Baby Bust" generation are a different breed from those who came before. Among their core values:

1. *Impatience.* The younger generation, like every generation before them, yearns for the good life. Because they grew up in a fast-paced society, they look for rapid advancement. They want as much as possible as fast as possible.

2. *Autonomy.* Baby Busters are far more likely than their elders to ask "What's in it for me?" They will give you their loyalty, but only if you can show them how loyalty to the company serves their personal interests.

3. *Self-Fulfillment.* They're looking for jobs that allow them to work at the things they enjoy, while allowing them the leisure to pursue off-

the-job interests. They are likely to see their jobs as means to an end — the end being a high-quality life full of fun and enjoyment.

4. *Cynicism.* They think the preceding generations have handed them a raw deal in the form of messy world problems and a sluggish economy that shows few signs of catching fire. They fear that their generation will never be as well off as their parents' generation.

5. *Extended adolescence.* A high percentage of them are products of broken homes, and grew up with absentee, workaholic parents. As a result, they tend to marry later, stay in college, and live with their parents longer.

6. *A need for attention.* The modern world has been tough on family life, and many Baby Busters are products of broken homes. They may feel that they have been cheated out of a normal childhood, so many of them look for managers and supervisors who can give them the time and attention their parents were unable to give them.

7. *Self-Reliance.* Often left to themselves by working parents, they've learned to make decisions on their own. Therefore, they're less likely to be impressed by the institutional authority represented by managers and supervisors.[4]

Of course, these characteristics do not describe all members of the rising generation, but they do show a decided generational shift in attitudes. Businesses that plan to succeed must take this shift into account. Giving these young people fundamental skills and technical know-how is certainly necessary. But helping them achieve productive, quality-conscious, winning attitudes is even more important. They must be shown how working toward corporate objectives can help them achieve their goals in life. And they must become quality conscious through the fifth pillar: an educational process that produces a quality-oriented culture.

Businesses must not only make unprecedented investments in employee education to produce a quality work force; they must also provide education for managers and supervisors who must deal with these newcomers. The new workers cannot be effectively bossed. They will require skillful coaching and mentoring by leaders with strong people skills. And how will your leaders acquire these "soft skills"? Only through a well-planned educational process.

No Way Around It

There is no way your company can escape this necessity. The new generation presents the business world with a sharp reduction in working-age population. There were 41 million Americans in their 20s in 1980. The figure for 2000 is estimated at 34 million. As the Baby Boomers reach retirement age, American business will face a dwindling pool of talent, with a different set of values. It will require a massive educational effort to mold these newcomers into a work force capable of taking on the world. But it can be done, and enlightened human-resource professionals are eager to tackle the job if you give them the resources.

In the past, only a small minority of American businesses have made significant investments in employee development. According to the American Society for Training and Development, American employers entered the decade of the '90s spending $30 billion a year on training and development. But the ASTD reports that 90% of that investment was made by only .05% of employers. That means that, on average, only one employer in 2,000 is making a meaningful investment in human assets.

Leading-edge companies now are spending at least 3.2% of total payroll on education and development, and some are spending significantly more. This is money well spent if it is invested in upgrading the individual as well as upgrading the individual's skills.

But the knowledgeable people in your human-resources department will tell you that it's money largely wasted if it is spent solely on teaching people how to do things.

CHARACTERISTICS OF A GOOD EDUCATIONAL PROCESS

What should you be looking for in an educational and development process?

Here are some necessary characteristics as I see them after working for more than 20 years helping companies to conceptualize, create and execute effective educational systems:

- *A comprehensive curriculum.* Don't concentrate on a narrow range of skills. Help all individuals in your organization to grow to their highest levels. An engineering company, for instance, may be tempted to devote its entire budget to hard skills and pay little attention to the sales side. But how often could the company make good use of an engineer's expertise in making a sales presentation?

If you ask the people at INA Bearing, the world's largest manufacturer of needle bearings, they'll tell you "quite often." INA educates its engineers in such non-technical areas as selling, presentation skills, and human behavior. When INA's salespeople need technical help with customers, they don't hesitate to call in the engineers. They know they have the people skills to do the job.

An engineer educated in sales techniques might be the ideal person to accompany your ace salesperson on a call.

- *Learning as a continuum.* Hit-and-run programs won't equip your business for the competitive climate of the new century. Your education and development process must follow a clear plan that shows how to get from Point A to Point B efficiently and profitably.

- *Teaching that is integrated, not segmented.* Companies commonly make the mistake of teaching one segment of employees but not teaching another. For example, they may educate their salespeople but not the sales manager. When this happens, the salesperson comes back from the course full of new ideas and brimming with enthusiasm. But the sales manager has received none of this input, and therefore is not ready to encourage or even to accept the new ideas and methods. The salesperson soon realizes this and stops trying to innovate. The educational effort has gone for naught. To be truly effective, education must reach each level of your organization with the appropriate learning.

- *On-the-job application.* A good educational program must show participants how to apply on the job what they learn in the classroom. Learning is no good unless it is applied on the job. The sixth pillar of your educational system will promote this on-the-job application, thereby helping employees to contribute to corporate performance, productivity and profitability.

- *Content equity.* Many executives elect to buy off-the-shelf programs on the assumption that there's no need to reinvent the wheel. But if you're buying a ready-made program, you're not building your content equity. To be effective, an educational program must communicate to your employees who you are and what you do that makes you unique. Off-the-shelf programs must, of necessity, be generic in nature. Your educational and development process should ensure that what your employees learn is in keeping with your philosophy, vision and corporate culture. It must provide the seventh pillar — education that reinforces your differential advantage. You can't buy that kind of focus off the shelf.

- *Credible leadership.* Management expert Joseph Juran once cautioned against using subordinates to teach senior managers. Senior managers often find it hard to take seriously the learning they receive from people several steps down the corporate chart from them. If you have a $30,000-a-year member of your education and development staff teaching a class of top executives, you may have problems of perception. It is critical that the program be led by a person who can command the respect and the commitment of top management. If you have no one in house who is capable of dealing with senior management as a peer, it may be advisable to hire an external consultant who has the needed stature and prestige.

- *Repetition.* Simple tasks may be taught in one session. If you have an employee who needs to master a simple technique, a one-time seminar may be all you need. But if you're trying to modify behavior through a change in mindsets, the one-time seminar won't do it. To quote Aristotle, "We are what we repeatedly do. Excellence, then, is not an act but a habit." New habits must be inculcated. To *inculcate* means *to teach and impress by frequent repetitions; to urge on or fix in the mind.* You will need to institute a process that continually reinforces the attitudes you want to inculcate until they become a part of the work-place culture.

MACHINE OR ORGANISM?

The need for education in the work place does not arise from some transient development in the business world. It stems from a whole new way of looking at the corporation and the social order of which it is a part, and it ties in with our emergence from the machine age into the knowledge age.

In the old perception, an organization followed a mechanical arrangement. So it could be compared to a machine.

Today's organizations need to be more like organisms. An organism is a living, developing thing. It's a thinking, adaptable organization.

Machines function by doing the same thing over and over. In a gasoline engine, for instance, the pistons move up and down in an unvarying pattern, propelled by explosions in the combustion chamber that follow the same sequence and the same timing, revolution after revolution. When a machine varies from the status quo, something is amiss, and the mechanic must find a way to return it to normal.

In old-style corporations, this type of repetition was considered the ideal. The way to succeed was to find a norm that worked. Henry Ford built his fortune by building an automobile that remained virtually unchanged year after year.

The mechanistic approach works so long as conditions remain stable. But when the market changes — when people's needs or preferences change because of new conditions or new possibilities — the mechanistic way falls short.

With today's knowledge explosion, people are constantly exposed to new products and new possibilities. Hence the demands of the marketplace are in a constant state of change. Corporations that continue to operate as machines will learn very quickly that you can't succeed anymore by maintaining the status quo.

In such mechanistic organizations, change is met by hostility and defensiveness, as people fight to retain old ways and to defend old turfs.

Mechanistic practices must give way to innovative thinking that sees a business not as a machine but as a living, developing organism. This thinking can be achieved only through an educational program that changes people from within.

Pause for a few moments and take a thoughtful look at your company and its people. Would you describe it as a thinking organism or a mechanistic organization? A few clues on the next pages will help you decide.

If your corporation leans toward the mechanistic mode, it's time to begin attacking the status-quo attitude through a well-planned, comprehensive educational program.

The rest of this book will be devoted to showing you how to do it. Let's begin by examining the first of the seven pillars: the education of the whole individual.

MECHANIST ORGANIZATION

- New ideas and methods are discouraged because they vary from the mechanical norm: "We've never done it that way before."
- Managers and supervisors rely solely on their own judgments, backed by the policy manuals, instead of empowering their people to make on-the-spot judgments that might improve quality and service.
- Employees hesitate to try novel approaches to tasks, processes and product development for fear of violating rigid procedures.
- Communication flows "through channels" rather than spreading throughout the business organization.

THINKING ORGANIZATION

- People at all levels can talk directly to people in other departments and divisions, and to customers and suppliers.
- Teams are formed across departmental lines, including employees at all levels, to execute new projects or to solve common problems.
- Line employees are routinely asked for their opinions and rewarded for ideas that work.
- Failures at innovative projects are regarded as learning experiences and not as black marks against the person who failed.
- Corporate structures are flexible and therefore able to adapt to the stress of innovation.

CHAPTER THREE

PILLAR ONE: EDUCATING THE WHOLE INDIVIDUAL

Your workers should not be robots, programmed for specific functions. They should be many-sided individuals with the potential to contribute to your profitability in many ways. Therefore, in developing your work force, it's a mistake to train people to become expert in just one area.

TECHNICIANS WHO CAN SELL

The Japanese learned that many years ago. When the Mazda automobile company experienced slack sales, it took people off the production line and put them on the sales force. With some education in sales techniques, these workers made excellent sales-people. They knew the product from the inside out, and could explain its virtues to customers.

The Daichi electronics store in Tokyo uses its service and repair people to generate new sales. Daichi gives a three-year warranty on the products it sells — two years longer than the manufacturer's warranty. The store keeps a record of its sales, and just before the warranty expires, the customer gets a telephone call. Daichi offers to send a technician to examine the product and make any needed repairs while it is still under warranty.

While still in the home, the technician offers to inspect any other appliances, regardless of whether they were purchased from Daichi.

The technician returns to the store and reports on the age and condition of every appliance in the house. At the appropriate time, the owners of an aging refrigerator or VCR will receive a call inviting them to visit the Daichi store and inspect the latest models.

Daichi technicians are much more than repair persons. They are well-rounded, educated represen-tatives of the store, with skills in sales, customer service, public relations and many other areas that promote profitability in their business.

FAST, FLEXIBLE, FOCUSED, AND FRIENDLY

Your organization cannot be content with im-parting superficial knowledge in narrow, specific skills. Rosabeth Moss Kanter, author and Harvard professor of business administration, has given us the formula for success in the 21st century: A company has to be fast, flexible, focused and friendly. To cultivate these qualities, your work force has to be versatile, innovative and proficient in people skills.

In addition to training people in specific skills, you need to teach them *how to obtain* the knowledge and skills they need to do their jobs. You want them to be *motivated* to apply their knowledge and skills toward achievement of corporate goals. You want them to know how to *mobilize* their knowledge and skills in the most productive ways.

LEARNING TO LEARN

An anonymous sage once ventured that "Education is what you have left over after you have forgotten everything you've learned."

That's a powerful insight. With education, learning becomes a renewable resource. An educated individual is like a spring, with its internal sources of water. As a spring replenishes itself when water is withdrawn, so educated individuals replenish their learning when existing knowledge has served its purpose.

An individual who has been trained but not educated is like a dipper. A dipper gets its water from an external source, and when the water's gone it can't refill itself. A trained individual acquires skills from an outside source and, when the skills are outdated, can't replace them without outside help.

Education involves teaching people to learn. At the height of the industrial age, the ability to learn was not considered essential. The tasks in the industrial process were broken into minute subtasks, which individuals were to perform repetitively. A worker's job might have been to tighten specific nuts a specified number of turns as a product moved down the assembly line. Once the worker had learned that mechanical procedure, further learning was considered unnecessary.

This type of rote learning was the accepted pattern in all phases of work-force training. The trainee learned the right answer to the right question; the right response to the right stimulus. Since the corporation was regarded as a machine instead of an organism, there was no need to develop new answers and new responses. New variables would only throw the machine out of balance.

Today's organization is a different type of animal. It is different because:

- The marketplace is constantly forcing organizations to change the way they do business. Matthew Juechter, as chair of the Council of Governors, American Society for Training and Development, put it this way:

  We live in an era whose hallmark is change. Particularly in our organizations, change has pushed us to the edges of what we already know. We have discovered that knowledge is a precious resource, but that unless it is developed, it quickly becomes useless. The ability to learn purposefully from our work and the ability to foster others' learning have become critical new business skills. Building them has become a particular challenge for human-resource professionals.[1]

- The new marketplace demands that businesses be customer-oriented, not product-oriented. This means that everyone involved in the design, production, sale and delivery of a product or service must have the customer in mind. Like the Mazda production workers and the Daichi technicians, everyone who works for the company is a customer-service representative. This requires human-relations skills, not just mechanical or procedural skills.

- Participative management has replaced the old hierarchical command-and-control system. Participative management requires a new breed of employee and supervisor. Herbert Hoover once said that "Wisdom ofttimes consists of knowing what to do next." Under the command-and-control system, the worker looked to the supervisor for explicit instructions on what to do next. In today's democratic work place, the workers themselves are expected to plan and execute the next step.

VITAL CONNECTIONS

The new learning requirements of our era force us to take new approaches to employee development. We have learned, for instance, that, for most people, information is not stored long-term in isolated chunks that can be totally recalled at will. Instead, people remember how bits of information connect with other information they have. If they forget the connections, they forget the information.

This was not a serious problem so long as "learning" consisted of mastering certain mechanical skills that were performed repetitively. Since these tasks were performed day after day, there was no need for the information to be embedded in the memory through connections with other information.

But in the modern work place, the knowledge taken in must be used to generate more knowledge. The connections become vitally important. They allow workers to bridge between what they already know and what they need to know to achieve continuous improvement.

This means that businesses can't teach workers clear-cut rules for every task, observes Larry Mikulecky, professor of education at Indiana State University. It isn't enough to memorize "a handful of principles." Workers need to "internalize patterns, get feedback, and develop judgment."[2]

In effect, Professor Mikulecky is saying what I've been emphasizing all along to my clients, and what I've heard increasingly from corporate human-resources professionals: What the modern worker needs is *education* in addition to *training*.

MILKSHAKE, PIE AND DESSERT

I can give you a simple illustration of the pitfalls of narrow, superficial training as opposed to educating the whole person.

I once went to a fast-food outlet to indulge my sweet tooth.

"I'll have a chocolate milkshake and an apple turnover," I told the young woman at the counter.

She flashed me a bright smile, and asked, "Would you like a dessert with that?"

The young woman had been "trained" in what to say. But it was short-term training. She had not been educated to fit this short-term information into the larger pattern of customer service. A year later, she had undoubtedly forgotten the memorized line. Had she been *educated* to discern the customer's needs and to look for ways of meeting them, the information could have been fitted into any number of encounters in any number of business situations — and it would have served her well for a lifetime. Thus educated, she would not have asked a customer if he wanted dessert to go with his sweets.

CRITICAL, CREATIVE THINKING

To be able to "learn to learn," workers need to be educated to look at their jobs creatively. That is, they must constantly be looking for ways to improve the way they do things. They must always be alert for the better way and be open to new ideas. These skills are products of broad education.

Workers must also be educated in the art of critical thinking. They must learn to probe beneath the surface facts and to question the conventional wisdom.

Creative thinking is a powerful ally of critical thinking. Employees must learn how to examine problems from many perspectives and reframe them to develop innovative approaches. The type of knowledge necessary for this type of thinking is quite different from that necessary to turn wrenches, pull levers, or perform other rote tasks.

TACIT VS. EXPLICIT KNOWLEDGE

The Institute for Research on Learning (IRL) at Palo Alto, California, divides work-place knowledge into two categories — tacit knowledge and explicit knowledge.

Such things as job skills, design rules, procedures and rules of thumb fall under the category of "explicit knowledge." "Tacit knowledge," includes such attributes as intuition, expertise, common sense, and good judgment.

Photographers uses explicit knowledge in loading their cameras, setting up tripods and setting the exposures and timing. They use tacit knowledge in choosing the right lens, choosing the right camera angle, posing the subject, helping the subject relax, and choosing just the right moment to release the shutter.

Canadian photographer Yousuf Karsh, who won fame for his 1941 portrait of Winston Churchill, put it this way:

There is a brief moment when all there is in a man's mind and soul and spirit is reflected through his eyes, his hands, his attitude. This is the moment to record.

Explicit knowledge tells you how to prepare for the moment. Tacit knowledge tells you when the moment has arrived.

"We are good at thinking systematically about how to acquire explicit knowledge," says Susan Stucky, associate director of the IRL. "We divide a job into tasks, we do a task analysis, we divide the tasks into skills, and we design training to deliver the skills. But the truth is that, even after all that, we still have to teach people to do the actual work."[3]

Tacit knowledge can be crucial to communicating explicit knowledge, as a trainer named Pearl H. M. King once demonstrated.

She was called upon to develop a method of teaching workers in a hosiery mill to embroider stockings, using a technique called "linking."

It was a hard task to learn. Most workers required 18 to 36 months to become expert at it. Ninety percent of them quit before they learned the task.

A time-and-motion expert had attempted to develop a training procedure. He found that the experienced linkers couldn't describe what they did. So he watched them, and developed a procedure based on what he observed. The training failed.

Pearl King took a different approach. Instead of watching the workers, she decided to learn the task herself. It took her 26 days to learn to link slowly but accurately. In so doing, she discovered skills that the workers couldn't describe and the time-and-motion expert couldn't see.

The expert thought the workers' fingers were guided by visual cues alone. So he made large models of knitting fabric to help newcomers see the cues. King discovered that experienced linkers use tactile clues. As they worked with their fingers, they would feel the tension of the fabric as it passed through the machine.

The expert also assumed that the linker's left hand did most of the work. To an observer, the right hand did not seem to move. In fact, the right hand played the decisive role in the task.[4]

King developed a training program that reduced the learning curve to between four and seven months.

The time-and-motion expert could observe the movement of hands and fingers. He also knew the mechanical process involved in linking. All this was *explicit* knowledge. But he couldn't observe what was happening in the minds and in the nerve-endings of fingertips — the *tacit* knowledge.

Good communication skills, however, would enable a person who had mastered the tacit knowledge to pass it on to others, as King did.

Researchers at Palo Alto found that conventional training did little to equip people to use their tacit knowledge. They studied people in actual work settings — on shop floors, in business offices, and in classrooms. They discovered that when people encountered barriers — whether physical or social — they formed spontaneous, informal groups that shared knowledge, expertise and methods to overcome the barriers.

The workers, in short, were using their interactive skills to increase their knowledge and develop solutions to problems. They not only established working relationships; they also formed social relationships.

The people entering these informal groups were motivated by a desire to learn. This motivation — and the communication skills that enable them to interact — can be acquired through education.

THE MOTIVATION CHALLENGE

People will exert themselves to acquire knowledge and skills and to mobilize them in behalf of the company if they are properly motivated.

The skills are acquired through training. Motivation is something you build in through your educational process. The education must start with the leaders. They must learn how to create motivational environments.

As a management consultant, I have studied human motivation for a long time, and helped to interpret it for scores of America's finest corporations.

I can distill what I have learned into 10 basic principles:

1.   ALL PEOPLE ARE MOTIVATED.

Think about the water in your kitchen faucet. It is under pressure to get out. It is motivated, but it doesn't have the opportunity to pour until you open the valve. You don't provide it with the motivation; it is already full of motivation. All you do is give it the opportunity.

A lot of people are like that. They're ready to act energetically; the motivation is there. It's up to corporate leaders to provide the opportunity.

Now think of a mountain stream. It has lots of motivation. It rushes down the hillside, and if you leave it alone, it will keep going until it reaches the ocean. You don't have to motivate it.

But suppose you want that stream to turn a turbine. You have to channel its waters through a conduit that will focus the current on the blades of the turbine.

When you do that, you can use the water to run machinery or generate electricity. The stream is still following its motivation, but now its motivation is directed toward your objectives.

Many people in your company are like that stream. They have lots of motivation, but they need someone to show them how to channel it toward productive activities. Your education and development process should be your channeling mechanism.

2. PEOPLE DO THINGS FOR THEIR OWN REASONS; NOT FOR YOURS OR MINE.

You may want a salesperson gradually to move a customer out of the portfolio because the customer no longer fits your marketing strategy. Holding on to the customer is against the long-term interests of your company.

But the salesperson may be motivated to continue cross-selling the customer because, after all, that's the salesperson's job and that's what pays the orthodontist.

You may be saddened to learn that your salespersons think more of their teen-agers' teeth than they do of your company's long-term profitability, but that may well be the case.

If you want to move marginal customers out of your corporate portfolio, you'll have to give your salespeople reasons that harmonize with their personal interests. You must educate them to look for congruence between their interests and corporate interests.

3. THE KEY TO ALL EFFECTIVE
   MOTIVATION IS IDENTIFICATION.

The late Thomas P. (Tip) O'Neill, who served as speaker of the United States House of Representatives, used to say that "All politics is local."

That was his way of observing that people make decisions on the basis of the things that affect them personally.

That's why it won't work to tell your sales force to go out there and sell, sell, sell for good old ABC Enterprises.

You have to show them that selling for good old ABC is the way to make good things happen for themselves.

But let's think about this in the context of educating your work force.

Suppose your employees see the corporation not as some bloodless entity but as an important part of their lives.

Suppose they identify with it and its people as intimately as people tend to identify with their alma maters.

When you were in school, and your team lost, you felt it as *your* loss, even if you were just a spectator in the bleachers.

If you can help your employees to identify that intimately with your company, you truly will create a motivating environment for them.

The company will cease to be just an office building, a factory floor or an organizational chart. It will be an important and integral part of your employees' lives.

When something becomes personal, it becomes important. When your employees begin to identify with your company and what your company is, good things begin to happen.

When you begin to show them how improvements in the quality of your products and services relates to improvements in their quality of life, then you will have them on board.

4.   PEOPLE CHANGE BECAUSE OF PAIN.

When the pain of staying the same becomes greater than the pain of changing, people will change.

Robert Frey, CEO of Cin-Made, a small manufacturer of mailing tubes and composite cans, learned about the role of pain in forcing change.

He and a partner bought the company from a woman who had run it as a benevolent autocrat. Her generous policies eventually led to red ink, and she appealed to her employees to accept a pay cut. They refused, and she sold out.

After taking over as CEO, Frey put the situation bluntly to his employees: Either they accepted a pay cut or the company would go under and they would have no jobs.[5]

The employees didn't like the pay cuts, and they didn't like their hard-nosed new CEO, but they liked the prospect of unemployment even less. So they accepted Frey's proposal.

But Frey soon found that you can't run a company successfully while its employees are seething with resentment. The pain of this resentment motivated him to change: He instituted a profit-sharing plan that eventually compensated employees for the pay cuts, and he led the company through a transition to participative management.

Frey's conclusion:

People hate change. Change of any kind is a struggle with fear, anger, and uncertainty, a war against old habits, hidebound thinking, and entrenched interests. No company can change any faster than it can change the hearts and minds of its people, and the people who change fastest and best are the people who have no choice.[6]

Hearts are changed through education. Frey inherited a group of employees who had never enjoyed the advantages of a modern education and development program. They had been trained to do their jobs, but had not been educated in the advantages and responsibilities of an involved work force. As a result, both management and employees had to endure much more pain than was necessary. But pain provided the motivation for healthy change.

5. IF YOU PAY ATTENTION TO PEOPLE, THEY'LL PAY ATTENTION TO YOU.

That means listening to others and not just hearing them.

Listening is active; you have to involve yourself in what the speaker is saying, absorbing the message intellectually and emotionally. Hearing is passive. It calls for no reaction; no response.

If you listen to individuals long enough, they'll tell you what their concerns and problems are. It's a good way for management to get to know its people — not just by name, but also by their interests and aspirations.

Listening is one of those "soft skills" that has little to do with pulling levers, turning screws or following procedures, but a great deal to do with achieving performance, productivity and profitability in your business.

6. PRIDE IS A POWERFUL MOTIVATOR.

Everybody is proud of something. If you can find out what makes your people proud, you can use that insight to channel their motivation.

One of the things that should make them proud is the company itself.

If you can find ways to help your people identify intimately with your company, then they will work their hearts out for you because they want to be proud of the outfit they work for. Leaders educated in the creation of motivational environments can help generate this pride in the company. Employees educated in the company's vision, mission and values will follow such leadership enthusiastically, because the company's interests have personal meaning for them.

7. YOU CAN'T CHANGE PEOPLE; YOU CAN ONLY CHANGE THEIR BEHAVIORS.

A grocery store in California once tried to order its management people to be nice to the employees.

The managers were given 10 pennies each to place in their left pockets at the beginning of the day.

Each time they paid an employee a compliment, they were to move one penny into the right pocket. At the end of the day, all the pennies were expected to rest in right pockets.

What was the first concern of those managers?

Getting those pennies into the right pocket.

What do you think the employees thought when they heard a compliment, then saw the manager take a penny out of one pocket and put it into another?

Do you think the employees knew what was going on? Did they feel complimented, or did they feel patronized?

You can't change feelings by executive order. You have to do it gently, day by day through education and development, and by living the behavior you want to see in others. It's not a mechanical act, but an emotional involvement.

8. THE EMPLOYEE'S PERCEPTION BECOMES THE EXECUTIVE'S REALITY.

When you speak to employees, they don't respond to what you say; they respond to what they *understand* you to say.

When employees observe your behavior, they respond to what they *perceive* you to be doing, and will try to emulate you.

Suppose you send an employee to a developmental workshop or seminar and she comes back brimming with new ideas and information.

But you haven't been exposed to all this stimulating stuff, and so your behavior doesn't change.

The employee observes this and concludes that the behavior she sees in you is the behavior you want.

This may not be the case at all. You may want the employee to implement all these new ideas, but your employee's perception is the reality you get.

9. YOU CONSISTENTLY GET THE
   BEHAVIORS YOU CONSISTENTLY
   EXPECT AND REINFORCE.

Look for ways to reward employees for doing the things you want them to do.

The reward may take the form of financial incentives, prizes, or simply public recognition for a job well done.

Reinforcement can be positive or negative.

If employees learn that a certain type of behavior results in lower earnings, less favorable hours or less desirable sales territories, they'll adjust their behavioral patterns.

Sometimes the absence of a response can serve as reinforcement. Behavior that goes consistently unrewarded will eventually be discontinued.

10. WE ALL TEND TO JUDGE OURSELVES
    BY OUR MOTIVES; BUT WE JUDGE
    OTHERS BY THEIR ACTIONS.

Put another way, we're inclined to excuse in ourselves behavior that we find unacceptable in others.

When *your employees* are late for work, it's because they're irresponsible and have no interest in their jobs. When *you're* late for work, it's because you were attending to necessary details that had to be taken care of.

Corporate leaders should be careful not to make assumptions about the motives of employees. Even the employee who engages in the unacceptable behavior may not be aware of the true motives. Your leaders must be taught to deal with behavior, not motives. If an employee is consistently late and a supervisor is unwilling to tolerate such behavior, the supervisor need only point out the unacceptable behavior, state the consequences of the continued behavior, and be willing to impose the consequences. It's then up to the employee to deal with the motives.

These 10 principles should be deeply embedded in the subconscious minds of your managers and supervisors so that they form the basis for everyday interaction with employees. They should form the foundation of a continuing educational process that will help you channel your employees' motivations into activities that will propel your company toward the future it desires.

MOBILIZING FOR PERFORMANCE

Knowledge, expertise and motivation don't put the numbers on the bottom line. Performance does. That performance is achieved through mobilization of the knowledge, expertise and motivation in behalf of the company's interests.

In the successful business, the company's prosperity is everybody's responsibility, and everybody is authorized to take measures to promote it. At the Marriott Corporation, for instance, employees — now called associates — are authorized to make decisions on the spot without asking their supervisors. They are encouraged to take whatever reasonable steps are necessary to satisfy a customer. Marriott therefore mobilizes the problem-solving capacities of its entire work force rather than relying on the judgments of a few people at the top.

But these employees can't exercise that kind of responsibility without being educated in techniques of problem-solving and customer relations.

WHAT MAKES A STAR?

Knowledge workers also become more effective through education.

In Chapter One, I referred to a study of top performers among computer programmers at Bell Labs in California.

The study, conducted in the Bell Labs Switching Systems Business Unit, showed that 10% to 15% of the programmers were star performers, and that star performers outperformed average workers by a margin of 8 to 1. Think of the dividends to be realized by increasing the percentage of star performers to 25% or 30%.

The study identified nine work strategies that characterize star performers. None of them involves mechanical techniques. All of them are qualities that can be acquired through education. They are:

1. *Taking initiative:* accepting responsibility above and beyond your stated job, volunteering for additional activities, and promoting new ideas.

2. *Networking:* getting direct and immediate access to coworkers with technical expertise and sharing your own knowledge with those who need it.

3. *Self-management:* regulating your own work commitments, time, performance level, and career growth.

4. *Teamwork effectiveness:* assuming joint responsibility for work activities, coordinating efforts, and accomplishing shared goals with workers.

5. *Leadership:* formulating, stating, and building consensus on common goals and working to accomplish them.

6. *Followership:* helping the leader to accomplish the organization's goals and thinking for yourself rather than relying solely on managerial direction.

7. *Perspective:* seeing your job in its larger context and taking on other viewpoints, such as those of the customer, manager and work team.

8. *Show-and-tell:* presenting your ideas persuasively in written or oral form.

9. *Organizational savvy:* navigating the competing interests in an organization, be they individual or group, to promote cooperation, address conflicts, and get things done.

Star performers and their run-of-the-mill colleagues differed in two distinct ways:

- The way they *ranked* strategies.
- The way they *described* them.

Star performers considered initiative, technical competence and other cognitive abilities to be core competencies. Show-and-tell and organizational savvy were on the outer edge of their circle of importance.

Middle performers placed show-and-tell and organizational savvy at the core. While star performers were focused on performance, middle performers were focused on impressing management.

WHAT IS INITIATIVE?

Initiative meant one thing to star performers and quite another to the middle performers. One middle performer told of gathering and organizing source materials, including documents and software tools, for a project he was beginning with his group. Another described writing a memo to his superior about a software bug. Both thought they were showing initiative.

But star performers regarded these as routine actions. Of course you fix a software bug when you find it. Of course you prepare in advance for a project. So what else is new? To the stars, initiative involves creative actions that go beyond the routine.

WHEN DO YOU NETWORK?

Star performers and middle performers also showed marked differences in their attitudes toward networking. The middle performers waited until after they had encountered problems before looking around for someone who could provide help and support. The star performers built a network of helpers and supporters in advance, so that they could call on them immediately when needed.

Some middle performers also lacked perspective. They understood the functions of their specific jobs, but they did not relate their jobs to the overall mission of the company. Nor were they skilled at identifying with the viewpoints of customers, managers or fellow members of the work team.

The study concluded that "Individual productivity . . . depends on the ability to channel one's expertise, creativity and insight into working with other professionals."

These are precisely the skills acquired through what the Institution for Research on Learning calls "tacit knowledge" and what we sometimes refer to as "the soft stuff."

GENERIC PROGRAMS WON'T DO IT

How can you educate your work force to reflect these qualities?

You can't do it through off-the-shelf programs that provide your employees with generic training and send them back to their work stations to apply the training on their own.

You can't do it by sending employees, individually or in groups, to out-of-town seminars where they sit with employees from other organizations and absorb the instruction, then return to an unchanged environment, among peers and supervisors who have not been exposed to the instruction.

EDUCATION CUSTOM-TAILORED FOR YOUR COMPANY

Your company is unique, and it needs an educational process tailored to its unique needs. You must identify the learning needs of your employees and construct an educational process that will address those needs.

You need to design a process that fits into your corporate culture and helps your employees identify with and become a part of that culture.

You need a process that will enable the employees to apply what they learn in their everyday jobs.

You need a process that educates employees and management, so that both are working from the same set of concepts and values.

And you need a process that will remain in place after the consultant who helped you design it has departed — a process that will leave the company with educational tools that it can apply in its journey of continuous improvement.

In short, your company needs to make education and development an element of its corporate culture. If you give your human-resources people the go-ahead to make education and development systemic, your organization will be able to adapt and flourish in the 21st century marketplace. If you restrict them to the provision of training that hasn't been enhanced by education, the organization will flounder in a constant struggle to update old skills to meet new demands.

But educating the individual is just one of the foundations on which good corporate education rests.

To be effective, an educational system must provide an integrated learning process for the entire organization. In the next chapter, we'll take a close look at this educational pillar.

CHAPTER FOUR

PILLAR TWO:
AN INTEGRATED LEARNING PROCESS

Do you think of your company as a machine or as an organism?

The way you think about it has a great deal to do with the way you manage it. A machine can be dealt with one part at a time. An organism demands an integrated approach, because its parts are interdependent and complementary.

Organisms differ from machines in many ways.

An organism is a living thing. It has the power to evolve, to transform itself, to change from within.

A machine is inanimate. It has no control over itself. It can respond only to outside controls.

Organisms can adapt to their environments. Machines can function only in fixed patterns.

Organisms can learn; machines can't.

If you expect your business to survive in an era of rapid change, you must transform it into a living, thinking, evolving organism. You must equip it to adapt to its changing environment and, indeed, to take the initiative in changing the environment itself.

A thinking organism must be able to do these five things very well:

1. Solve problems systematically.
2. Develop new products, new services and new approaches.
3. Learn from experience and from an examination of its own past.
4. Learn from others.
5. Spread what it learns throughout the work force.

When your company has made the switch from machine to organism, here's what it can do:

- Mobilize the expertise of people in all departments and at all levels in responding quickly to changing market conditions.

- Turn every employee into an agent of excellence with a commitment to customer service.

- Enable the entire organization to benefit from the expertise of the star performers.

- Unite all stakeholders — shareholders, employees, vendors — behind a common set of values, a common vision and mutually supportive goals.

AN INTEGRATED
EDUCATIONAL APPROACH

Turning your company into a healthy, vigorous, innovative organism requires an integrated educational approach. You can't educate just part of your organization, any more than you can educate just part of an individual. In football, kicking specialists are often referred to as having "educated toes," but the toe is only a minor part of the complex process that produces a successful field goal. The eyes, brain, legs, ankles, knees — practically every muscle and joint in the body — must know precisely what to do and the precise moment at which to do it if the kick is to split the uprights at the proper elevation.

A business organism requires a similar coordination among its components.

Each component must know not only what it is doing, but also what the other components are doing and what the organization as a whole is doing — and why. This pervasive knowledge enables all individuals and all units to be mutually supportive. It cannot be achieved through piecemeal training efforts.

PITFALLS OF THE PIECEMEAL
APPROACH

Three examples of piecemeal approaches will make the point.

Let's say that you send your sales staff off to out-of-town seminars one person at a time — perhaps as rewards for good performance. Each individual returns with a fund of new information and new ideas. But the employees return to the same environment, working with supervisors and colleagues who have not received the new knowledge. Gradually the new knowledge fades from disuse. The old ways prevail.

Now suppose you elected to educate your sales staff but you neglected to educate your sales manager. Your sales staff returns to the job brimming with new ideas and new approaches, but the sales manager has never heard of them. He has been drilled in the old ways and that's where his comfort zone lies. So gradually, the sales staff's new knowledge withers on the vine. Your education and development dollars were wasted.

Suppose you invest in an educational process for your entire sales department. But you neglect to educate your engineering, product-development, production, accounting and marketing people. Your products are designed by people who know very little about the marketplace. The people who plan them are largely in the dark about competing products, prices, customer needs or customer preferences. The people who make them know little about the purpose for which they are intended. Your marketing people know little about the purpose or the philosophy behind the design. Your accounting people know little about the resources that went into the development and production. Your organization, in short, doesn't know why it's making the product, who it's making it for, how much it costs to make it or how much you can charge your customers. You may have an excellent sales staff, educated in all the qualities that make good salespeople. But they won't be able to sell what you're producing.

A TRACTOR THAT COULDN'T PULL

The Chinese learned where this kind of narrow training could lead during the period before Deng Xiaoping opened up the mainland to Western ideas. The Chinese built their own tractors, designed by engineers who had been taught to build engines, transmissions and chassis. But these engineers had never worked on a farm and had never driven a farm tractor. So the tractors arrived without drawbars — which made them useless for pulling plows and other equipment.

Contrast that situation with the "boundaryless corporation" described by General Electric CEO Jack Welch:

In a boundaryless company, internal functions begin to blur. Engineering doesn't design a product and then "hand it off" to manufacturing. They form a team, along with marketing and sales, finance and the rest. Customer service? It's not somebody's job. It's everybody's job. Environmental protection in the plants? It's not the concern of some manager or department. Everyone's an environmentalist.

No Walls Between Functions

In today's organization, you can't build walls between functions. The parts of an organism must interact if the organism is to function well. Interaction requires shared knowledge, shared values, shared goals, and a shared commitment.

All of this requires a common culture, and culture is acquired through an educational process.

If you educate your line workers to function in a participative management environment, but don't teach your supervisors how to delegate and confer authority, you are headed for deep trouble.

If you teach your supervisors to delegate, but don't prepare your line workers to assume responsibility and make decisions, you are on the road to disaster.

If you want an innovative, risk-taking corporate culture, you need to cultivate that mind-set among all your employees.

If you want your strategic planning to be guided by the corporate vision, your employees must be intimately familiar with the corporate vision. They must be taught to use it in their goal-setting. They must be taught to develop action plans that lead to fulfillment of the goals.

DON'T OVERLOOK ANYONE OR ANYTHING

A good education and development system overlooks no department and overlooks no facet of employee development.

Sales training, for example, is vital to every organization, because nothing happens unless something is sold. But sales training should not be confined to your sales staff, nor should the education of salespeople be restricted to sales training.

If your employees don't know what they're doing, don't believe in what they're doing, and don't take pride in what they're doing, the best sales force in the world won't be able to move your products.

THE SALES-PRODUCTION CONNECTION

Let us suppose your sales people think only about sales and your production people think only about production. Your company could easily be thrown off balance. Too often, when a company experiences excess capacity — when sales are slack and production is booming — the production people rest on their laurels and wait for the sales effort to catch up. The sales people are so busy trying to drum up sales that they don't ask themselves how much sales volume the production department can sustain.

Then, when sales are booming, and orders are backlogged to the horizon, production people have no time to think about improving production; everybody is concentrating on filling current orders with current methods and equipment. When sales and production people talk knowledgeably to one another, they can anticipate periods of glut and slack and make plans for dealing with them. They can talk knowledgeably to one another when the people in each department have received broad educations in the company's values, mission and strategy.

NAY-SAYERS OR ENABLERS?

Your financial people, too, need a clear understanding of their relationship to the company and its goals. Too often, financial people see themselves as keepers of the treasury chest, whose jobs are to find as many reasons as possible to say "no" to expenditures. Through education, they can be brought aboard the corporate team, and initiated into the process of finding new ways to meet the challenges of change while maintaining fiscal responsibility. Lee Iacocca, when he was head of the Ford Division, had to fight the "bean counters" all the way to the showroom before he could introduce the Mustang — one of the most successful new cars in history.

EXPANDING HORIZONS

On the production line, workers not only need to know *how* to perform their assigned tasks; they also need to know *why* they perform them. They need to understand how their tasks fit into the overall process, and how they contribute toward company goals.

The old assembly-line mentality severely restricted employees' views of their corporate roles. Dr. Elliot Jacques, whose discipline is social relations, has noted that people at different levels of the corporate hierarchy work within different time horizons. Hourly workers, he said, have an hour's or a day's time horizon. Supervisors look ahead a month or so. Managers may think ahead a year or five years. Leaders, he said, work within a 25-year time horizon.

An educational system can broaden the time horizons of your employees so that they're working in the long-term interests of your company.

Think about it: Your line workers are in better position than anyone else to influence your long-term interests. They control the processes that absorb most of your input and produce all your output.

PUTTING INNOVATION ON THE LINE

My valued friend and colleague, Dr. Charles Dygert, is a leading exponent of participative management, and he provides an excellent example of the benefits of education at the level of the line employee.

Charlie tells about a plant in Ohio engaged in the manufacture of axles for big trucks. The business end of the process was a huge press that stamped out axle halves. When it came time to retool the press, the plant had to be shut down for 12 hours.

One day, some of the hourly workers approached the plant manager and told him they believed that, with some special tooling, the down time could be reduced to only a few minutes. The plant manager listened. Their idea sounded workable. He tried it, and as a result, the periodic retooling was accomplished in just over 14 minutes.

The idea saved more than time. Charlie Dygert estimated the cost of downtime in a major plant at $10,000 a minute. At that rate, the employees' idea saved the company more than $7 million each time the press had to be retooled.

The employees came forward, Charlie points out, because they had bought into the goals and principles of the company. They had been educated to see themselves not as machine operators but as agents of the company.

ATTITUDINAL CHANGE IN ENGLAND

Another excellent example comes to us from England, where the electric power industry was privatized several years ago. Because of the heavy expense of decommissioning old nuclear plants, the nuclear segment of the industry was organized into Nuclear Electric, a government-owned company, receiving decreasing subsidies each year until it could make a profit on its own.

On one occasion, company officials watched as steam vented from a valve on the roof of a building at the Hartlepool Power Station, indicating that a minor malfunction had shut down one of the two reactors. The company would lose two days of power generation at a cost of $1.4 million in revenue.

"A few years ago, a cheer went up when one of the reactors tripped," remarked one official. "It was a chance to string the job out and get as much overtime as you possibly could."

Now when a reactor trips, the employees get busy finding the cause and returning the unit to service.

The change in attitude resulted from a culture change through which employees learned to identify their own interests with the interests of the company.

Part of it involved financial incentives: The company began rewarding employees when it achieved its target output.

But management gives major credit to an attitudinal change brought about through a sharing of information with employees and the removal of communication barriers. Plant Manager Tony Capp confided to his staff that the station was in danger of losing up to $125.5 million that year. Immediate change was inescapable. The staff conveyed the situation to the entire work force.

Capp eliminated barriers to communication in a number of ways:

- Whereas engineers had traditionally worn white uniforms while line workers wore blue, he ordered a single color for all employees.

- The partition was torn down between the management and employee dining rooms.

- Special parking spaces for senior management were abolished.

- People at each level in the organization were taught to perform the tasks that had been performed by people at the next highest level. Thus, production workers were able to relieve engineers of much of their repetitive work.

The results were dramatic. In 1992, the station increased its power production by 40% over the previous year and income from the sale of that output rose 31%. The station was able to cut costs so that its overall contribution to Nuclear Electric rose by 88%.[1]

Note that this improved performance resulted from a combination of three things:

- *Financial incentives* that channeled employee motivation in the direction of company goals.

- *Training* in the skills required at the next level on the corporate ladder.

- *Education* regarding the necessity for change and the attitudes necessary to effect the change.

Education as the Vehicle for Change

Cultural change can be effected only through an educational process that permeates the organization. The educational process becomes the vehicle for change.

There is a certain inertia that characterizes individuals and organizations. We don't want to change unless some outside force or circumstance interferes with the status quo. Physicists tell us that an object at rest will remain at rest until it is acted upon by an outside force. An object in motion will remain in motion unless it is acted upon by an outside force.

The same is true of organizations and individuals. Some prefer a stable, unchanging environment. Others embrace constant change.

To be successful in the 21st century, businesses must make change a natural characteristic. Change must be as natural for your company as motion is for the earth and its planetary siblings.

Educating Management for Change

The change must be led by top management. If top management doesn't change, the company doesn't change. So successful leaders must learn to anticipate the need for change and to lead others in bringing about positive change.

You don't just go down to the plant one day and say, "Listen up, folks: We're going to have a cultural change and you're all going to be a part of participative management."

Change requires an educational process among people at all levels of the corporation. Managers and supervisors must be taught to accommodate change. They must learn to develop strategies for coping with change. They must learn to cultivate a sense of humor in coaching employees through the change. They must unlearn some old assumptions. Among them:

- Yesterday's solutions will solve today's problems.
- Present trends will continue.
- There's no use planning on the basis of changes the future might bring.

Managers must also learn to develop a nose for news, which will enable them to keep up with the latest methods and trends. They must learn to bid good-bye to the past, with all its outdated baggage, and look to the future with confidence in their success.

A corporate aptitude for change is acquired through an educational process. This doesn't mean that technical training is not important. Technical competence is a pre-requisite for success in any undertaking, but it only gets you into the game. To win, you need the extra qualities that education imparts.

EDUCATING FOR CREATIVITY

High up on the list of those qualities is creativity — a corporate asset that can be cultivated through education.

Creative people are not afraid to challenge tradition. "Because that's the way it's always been done" is an unsatisfactory answer for them. If it's always been done a certain way, that's reason enough for them to look for a better way.

Creative people have learned to look at the world from the perspective of the character in the George Bernard Shaw play who said: "You see things; and you say, 'Why?' But I dream things that never were; and I say, 'Why not?'"

Creative people are always looking for ways to improve what's there. They look at things from new and different perspectives, always looking for what isn't quite right or what might be made better.

These are teachable attributes that become part of the corporate mentality when they are inculcated through a continuous educational program.

INDICATORS OF NEEDED CHANGE

The need for change in your organization may be indicated by a number of signs. Among them:

- You've been following the same policies and procedures for longer than two years.

With change occurring so rapidly, it's likely that a better way of doing things has been developed over the past two years. Expanding knowledge and resources are constantly creating better opportunities. Look at your procedures and ask yourself, "How would we do this today if we were starting all over?"

- Managers are not delegating responsibilities.

This is a sure sign that participative management has not taken hold and that creativity within this area of responsibility is being bottled up by an authoritarian management system. The manager needs to consider a change in leadership styles and a plan for developing the work force's capacity for self direction.

- Your employees are in the NIH (Not Invented Here) syndrome, ignoring fresh ideas that might be learned from competitors or other outside sources.

This is an indication that the corporation is closing its eyes to innovative thinking in the industry. The business that refuses to learn from other businesses will soon find itself in a class by itself — at the bottom of the scale.

- Your people are convinced that their way of thinking is the only way.

This is the attitude that "There's a right way, a wrong way and the company's way." Your people must learn to substitute "a better way" for "the company's way." Unless they're constantly looking for that better way, they'll never progress.

Sometimes the need for change is more obvious. Leaders may undertake major changes for the following reasons:

- *Something has gone wrong and the system needs to be returned to equilibrium.* The leader approaches this change in a non-judgmental way. The object is not to find out who caused the problem but to find a way to rectify it.

- *Performance is chronically poor, and restructuring is necessary to improve it.* This may require the leader to identify cases in which people are temperamentally unsuited for their jobs. An extrovert may be stuck in an office all day dealing with lifeless figures when she would be better utilized out making contacts and lining up business. A prickly perfectionist might be alienating customers in a job requiring interaction with the public when he would be happier dealing with facts and figures, or manipulating software.

  Restructuring also may mean adjusting assignments and workloads when some people are overworked and others are underemployed. Managers educated in the "soft stuff" can learn to identify behavior styles and learning styles, and thus match the employee to the job.

- *Your organization has serious internal or external problems that won't yield to Band-Aid approaches.* In such cases, a thorough reorganization is required. This usually happens when the structural faults within the organization are too deep to yield to superficial approaches. The organization can't function smoothly without management's continuous intervention. It loses its external competitiveness because it wastes its energy handling internal problems.

MAKING CREATIVITY FLOWER

To bring about constructive change, your people must be able to think creatively.

Strategic planning is a powerful instrument for effecting the changes you want. But it calls for creative thinking. Creative thinking is not an inborn characteristic. It is one of those "soft skills" that can be imparted through a continuing education process.

Creativity will *flower* if you cultivate these qualities in your people:

F lexibility

L earning

O penness to alternatives

W onder

E agerness for the future

R eadiness to test ideas

FLEXIBILITY

Flexible people never become married to an idea. If a creative direction leads to a dead end, they're not afraid to acknowledge that they're at a dead end and look for another creative direction. They're constantly abandoning ideas that don't work and continuing their search for ideas that do work. They turn their failures into learning experiences and build upon them.

LEARNING

Creative people have a thirst for knowledge. They like to read, travel and explore. They browse through libraries, book stores, and magazine racks. They enjoy new places and new experiences. They like to get off the Interstates and explore the byways. They like to pick other people's brains. The stockpile of knowledge and experiences they accumulate becomes a fertile source of creativity.

OPENNESS TO ALTERNATIVES

Creative people don't feel threatened by new ideas, whatever their source. They're not afraid to borrow ideas from others. They read about other people's experiments, and thus learn what methods to emulate and what mistakes to avoid. Creative people find as many alternatives as possible, then determine logically which alternative to pursue.

WONDER

A childlike sense of wonder is essential to creativity. The great discoveries of the universe have been made by people who asked questions children ask and looked for the answers. Isaac Newton, according to legend, propounded the law of gravity after being hit by an apple that fell from a tree. He asked the question, "Why did the apple fall down instead of falling up?" Albert Einstein gained insight into the nature of gravity when he asked, "Why don't we feel gravity while we're falling?" His theories of relativity rested upon such childlike questions as "Does the train pull away from the station, or does the station pull away from the train?"

EAGERNESS FOR THE FUTURE

Creative people look at the future as a big adventure instead of a looming threat. They're not afraid to bid good-bye to the status quo and embrace new practices. They are eager to seize the opportunities the future brings.

READINESS TO TEST IDEAS

Creative people know that not all ideas are feasible or practical. They look at them objectively to determine their value. They test them on a small scale before implementing them on a large scale.

Each of these qualities can be cultivated through education.

IMPLEMENTING CHANGE

The company that implements a cultural change needs to be educated in the process of change. Management must know how to guide its employees through the difficult transition from the old way to the new one. Change cannot be implemented overnight. It has to be carefully planned and executed.

When the environmental controls group of the giant Johnson Controls restructured its divisions, its management invited me to keynote a four-day conference in Scottsdale, Arizona. The group was in the process of abolishing its divisional lines and redesigning the delivery of products and services to the market. It held several intensive briefings to study, absorb and understand the impact of change.

I watched in admiration as the sales and management teams worked together, making constructive use of the "soft skills" acquired through the company's educational process.

One thing should be remembered when you're embarking on a major transition: People hunger for stability amid change.

The steady, reliable people in any organization are often fearful of change. Management must keep them in mind. You must assure them that change doesn't mean an end to their world; it means a continuation, but with improvements.

Here are some things you can do:

- Explain the reasons for the change. When people understand the logic behind change, it becomes more rational and more comfortable.

- Show how your plans keep risks to a minimum.

- Emphasize the things that will remain the same.

- Let people know what to expect, step by step. Don't surprise them.

- Let people know that management is fully behind the change. Your confidence in the value of the changes will be reassuring to them.

- Commend them and recognize them for the constructive changes they make.

EDUCATING IN CORPORATE VALUES

Successful changes are based on values and are in harmony with the corporate vision and mission.

Values provide a common language for the company's leaders and its people, and make it easier to align everyone behind the common purpose. Employees must be educated in the company's values before they can buy into the company's vision and goals.

A THREE-STAGE PROCESS

Planned change involves a three-stage process: softening, reshaping and restabilizing.

SOFTENING

The softening stage is the most uncomfortable for employees. After years of doing things the same old way, they have been hardened into rigid habits. Now they have to unlearn them. This may require that behavior that was once acceptable and even rewardable now become stigmatized. To accomplish the softening, you'll need corporate leaders educated in the management of change. Management can then implement an educational process to help employees reorient their behavior.

This is the time when it pays to know your people.

Not all people have the same tolerance level for change. Some people seem to be brave and tough, but they're just putting on a front to hide their feelings of inadequacy. This is where managers need the people skills that only a good corporate educational program can provide. They need to get out and talk to people to find out what's been happening in their lives, what they think about it and how they've responded to it. Only then can they provide sensitive, intelligent guidance through the softening.

One of the greatest fears associated with change is the loss of personal identity. You can help prepare your employees by letting them know what roles they will be playing and what functions they will be performing after the change. In other words, tell them who and what they will be.

It is essential that you provide people with the information they'll need to adjust to the change. Make clear the reasons for change and the consequences of not changing. Emphasize the opportunities that the change opens up for employees. Both the gain and the pain must be made clear.

RESHAPING

The reshaping phase calls for a positive educational approach. We're now less concerned with rooting out old ways and more concerned with implanting new ways. Managers and employees must be convinced that the new way is the right way.

Compensation and reward systems must be redesigned to reflect the new values and to encourage new behaviors.

During this period, leaders must be personally involved in implementing the change. They must monitor the change carefully to determine what's working and what isn't.

This is a good time to involve your people in the change. If you give them an opportunity to help plan and implement the change, they are much more likely to buy into it.

RESTABILIZING

Finally comes the restabilizing stage. During this period, you want the new behaviors to become a natural part of the everyday routine in the work place. The new compensation and reward system is in place, and your work force has learned what behaviors will be rewarded. Now these behaviors must become a routine part of their daily work lives.

Here are some techniques for accomplishing this:

1. *Pilot projects.* Let employees try out new methods in "practice runs" to see how they work. This will help managers and employees feel comfortable and natural with the new ways when they're finally implemented.

2. *Provide suitable role models.* Find people who are familiar with the new ways and let them model them for the rest of your managers and employees. When your people witness the success of the new methods, they'll feel more comfortable about following them.

3. *Recognize and reward those who practice the new behaviors you want to encourage.* If you're asking people to value teamwork above individual

effort, for instance, then the system must be set up to reward team efforts.

EDUCATION AT EACH STAGE

Each stage in the process of change requires an educational process tailored to the needs of your company at that particular stage.

Throughout the change process, everyone from line workers to senior management must be convinced that the company is behind the change. Executives themselves must take responsibility for encouraging the new behavior. They must model it as they deal with people on as many levels as possible in the organization. Everyone in the organization plays a role in the change. All employees must be educated to fill their respective roles.

Once you have restabilized, don't regard the change as completed. In the modern management world, change is not a program with a beginning and an end. It is a never-ending process. When you have stabilized after one change, it's time to look ahead and lay the groundwork for the next round of improvements.

CREATING A SHARED VISION

To look ahead that far, you need to have a vision of the company's future: What will it look like five years, 10 years or 25 years down the road?

This vision will help you to focus your market, your customers, your products and your services. It will serve as the basis for your strategic planning.

The most effective visions are those in which all the company's stakeholders share in the creation. To achieve this broad input, your employees must be educated in such areas as group problem solving, values clarification, communication, and creative thinking. The "soft stuff" provides the matrix in which your company's future is created.

The vision must be more than a dry document that is published in the company newspaper and posted on a bulletin board. It must embody the shared values of the company's stakeholders. They must believe in it and act in harmony with it. Values are not the products of technical or procedural training. They are inner qualities that arise from an educated work force.

Look at the following values and ask yourself how your business would change if all your stakeholders bought into each of them:

- A passion for profits.
- Service to customers.
- Change for continuous improvement.
- Living by high ethical standards.
- Striving for excellence.
- Working safely.
- Rewarding and celebrating achievement.
- Valuing leaders.
- Encouraging working together.
- Valuing diversity.

- Respecting, supporting and empowering one another.
- Communicating openly and effectively.

These are the values adopted by the people at Du Pont Polymers. They can serve as the basis for a corporate vision. The entire corporation can then align itself behind the vision through divisional, departmental and team visions. A corporation thus aligned is in position to create its own future, charting a sure course through the treacherous currents of change.

Such alignment is achievable only when you are dealing with an organization guided by positive, creative attitudes that are the products of a continuing top-to-bottom educational process.

Such a process has to be planned and tailored to the specific needs of your company.

A consulting firm with savvy in corporate management and human-relations skills can guide you in creating the framework for such a process. But when the consultant leaves, your company should have a system in place that its own education and development staff can administer.

With such a system, technical and procedural training can still be delivered, for training will always be needed to teach repetitive skills and procedures.

But the fundamental task of your human-development program will be to provide your organization with comprehensive education in the skills and attitudes necessary to turn change into an instrument of profitability instead of the agent for obsolescence.

Management alone can't produce profitability in a business organization. The commitment of the entire work force is required. That's why it is important that your corporate educational system contain a pillar that supports an employee-management partnership. We will explore this educational pillar in the next chapter.

CHAPTER FIVE

PILLAR THREE: TURNING EMPLOYEES INTO PARTNERS

Do your employees work *for* you or *with* you?

The answer to that question will tell you a great deal about your company's ability to prosper in the era of change.

If your employees work *for* you, they will tend to do what you ask them to do and no more.

If they work *with* you, they will join you in the search for better methods, better ideas and higher profitability. They will be transformed from a group of passive order-takers into an organization of intelligent action-takers.

TURNING "US VS. THEM" INTO "WE"

More than a century ago, Henry Peter Brougham remarked that "Education makes people easy to lead, but difficult to drive; easy to govern, but impossible to enslave."

His observation is valid in the business as well as in the political world. An educated work force will form a partnership with intelligent leadership, but will not be driven. Turning your employees into partners requires attitudinal changes. If they are to behave as partners, they must learn to see themselves as part of the organization and not as hirelings who are paid to perform specific tasks. They must cultivate the *entrepreneurial* mentality as opposed to the *worker* mentality.

You can tell whether your employees regard themselves as partners or as hirelings by listening to them talk.

Do they refer to the company as "them" or as "us"? If the company is "them," then you have some educational tasks ahead of you.

BENEVOLENT POLICIES ARE NOT ENOUGH

Benevolent company policies alone won't accomplish this attitudinal change. This is the lesson Robert Frey learned after he and a partner bought Cin-Made, the Cincinnati composite-can manufacturer.

"The kind of change we experienced doesn't come simply from treating people well," he asserted.

The previous owner had gone out of her way to treat people well.

"She saw her employees as family," Frey observed. "She threw costume parties for them. She loved listening to their personal problems, she kept track of their kids, and she showed them a good deal of loyalty. Among other things, she kept people on the payroll when she should have let them go. When she did fire people, she'd have second thoughts and hire them back again. She knew what was best for her people, and she made sure they got what they needed."[1]

But when she asked her employees to cut her a little slack because their overly generous pay scale was driving her toward bankruptcy, the employees balked. The company's financial predicament was her problem, not theirs. To them, the company was "them" and its employees were "us."

Frey's hard-line insistence on a substantial cut in pay and benefits deepened the "us vs. them" division within the company. The employees accepted the cut, because they had little choice, but it left them angry and disgruntled.

"As that year passed, I realized with increasing clarity that our victory was not making me a happy man or a successful business owner," he said. "I knew that the company would never succeed, perhaps not even survive, unless we all gave it the same total commitment. But the workers didn't see Cin-Made as their company; they saw it as the owners' company. That had to change. I didn't want to be their worthy adversary; I wanted to be their worthy partner."[2]

SHARING PROFITS AND PAIN

So Frey decided to share the company with the employees.

"In the beginning, it was the pain I wanted to share as much as the profit. I wanted the workers to worry. Did any one of them ever spend a moment on a weekend wondering how the company was doing, asking herself if she'd made the right decisions the week before?"[3]

So he implemented a profit-sharing plan. He also introduced participative management. Frey had to lean on his managers to empower the employees to exercise more individual responsibility, and he had to lean on his employees to accept the responsibility.

Gradually, the company recovered, making progress in quality, profitability, and employee/management relations.

EITHER BUT NOT BOTH

The acid test came when a group of hourly employees demanded a pay raise in addition to the profit sharing.

Frey told them they could have either a raise or profit-sharing, but not both.

"If you choose the raise, I'll match the best percentage increase your union can negotiate anywhere in the country with any employer," he told them. But he would keep the difference between what the employees would get in raises and what they might have gotten in profit sharing, because "all the risk will be mine again." The employees compared their profit-sharing benefits with the pay increases other companies were granting and decided to stick with profit sharing.[4]

EDUCATION FOR NEW RELATIONSHIPS

Turning employees into partners requires a high level of education on the part of management and employees. It calls for new types of relationships, and the new relationships must be learned by people at all levels.

Here are some of the goals your educational strategy must accomplish:

1. It must align management and employees behind the corporate vision, supported by corporate, departmental and individual goals.

2. It must identify and inculcate corporate values.

3. It must help management and employees identify and embrace the corporate mission.

4. It must educate managers and supervisors for their new roles as coaches and facilitators instead of transmitters of orders.

5. It must educate line workers to see their roles as creators of value rather than performers of rote functions.

6. It must help workers acquire the skills needed for self-management, including team-building, planning, goal-setting, problem-solving, conflict resolution, negotiating, and risk-taking.

If you do just one of those things, you're spitting into the wind. If you do just five of the six, you're severely limiting your chances of success. A good educational process will address all these needs in an integrated fashion. It will set up a system that will continually promote a unifying body of values, attitudes and behaviors.

INCULCATING THE VISION AND MISSION

A corporate *vision* is the company's mental picture of the future it desires. For the vision to be effective, it must permeate the consciousness of the entire work force. The company's *mission* is closely related to the vision. It is a simple but eloquent statement of the way the company proposes to fulfill its vision.

A vision is not something top management dreams up and presents to its employees with the announcement, "This is what we're going to achieve."

INDENTIFYING CORPORATE VALUES

Effective visions must spring from corporate values the employees themselves can embrace willingly.

Not all employees, of course, will subscribe to the same values. For instance, your corporate values may include a deep concern for the environment.

Some of your employees may believe that environmental concerns are overblown and that economic interests should not be sacrificed for the sake of a pristine environment. Such employees should be free to follow their own values on their own time. But while they are involved in company activities, you have a right to require them to base their decisions on company values. That means that you must provide a good educational grounding in corporate values.

Conflicting values should not be a major problem if the company has sought broad input into values identification. Corporate values should not reflect the personal idiosyncrasies of the CEO. They should have a broad base of support within the organization, and they should be consistent with the overall purpose of the company.

Where company values conflict with personal values, it's best not to give the individuals either/or choices. Rather, management should look for alternatives that will violate neither set of values. This enables individuals to hold on to their own values while supporting company objectives.

The mission statement provides the conceptual framework within which the company proposes to fulfill its vision while adhering to its values. Employees should be thoroughly familiar with the mission statement, for it provides a straight-edge to guide long-range planning and day-to-day decision-making.

The vision, values and mission statement are the fundamental tools for shaping corporate culture. They underlie all the company's rules, policies and guidelines. The only way they can be employed effectively is through a thorough, well-thought-out educational process.

HOW DUKE POWER CHANGED ITS CULTURE

To get an idea of how the process works, let's look at the way Duke Power Company, a large utility headquartered in my home state of North Carolina, approached its transition to participative management over a six-year period.

Duke first dispatched a middle-management team to examine the methods of companies noted for the vibrancy of their corporate cultures. The team returned and submitted to management a proposed "Excellence Management Philosophy."

Top management then asked the team to draft a corporate vision, based on this philosophy, which would lead to the creation of a company they would find exciting to work for.

The team drafted the vision and a mission statement — a document showing how the company proposed to achieve the vision. It also drafted a set of "guiding principles," expressing the company's fundamental values.

The team then selected 600 employees from all levels of the company and sought their reactions through focus groups. The documents were revised to reflect this input and were resubmitted to top management. Management accepted them with only minor changes.

Then the company embarked on a two-year program aimed at educating its entire 19,400-person work force in the concept of corporate visions, missions and values. The aim was to teach the employees how to become accountable for their own lives and for the success of the corporation.

PARTICIPATION THROUGH TEAMS

Employees assume this accountability through participative management, which relies heavily on the team system. The team system relies on the collective efforts of workers who collaborate rather than compete with each other.

Several types of teams are used within the business setting.

Task forces are formed to explore specific issues. A corporate task force might be commissioned to explore ways of opening up opportunities to women and minorities. Or it might be asked to look for ways to control payroll expenses without mass layoffs. *Project-management* teams are often assigned to carry a project from start to completion. *Quality circles* may be formed to meet regularly and explore issues related to the quality of products and services. *Product-development teams* may be assigned to conceptualize and design new products. The success of each type of team depends on the ability of its individual members to participate in group problem-solving and decision-making. These abilities, in turn, rely heavily on the cultivation of good communication skills.

THE SELF-MANAGED TEAM

The self-managed team represents the ultimate in participative management. Many of the functions of management and supervision are often turned over to such teams.

Delta Airlines has let non-union workers select lead mechanics and quality-control supervisors for more than 30 years. Delta management screens candidates to make sure they meet company and Federal Aviation Administration requirements. Management also reserves the right to reject the workers' choice, although this rarely happens. Ninety percent of the time, the employees choose the same person that management would have picked.

At its Blue Ridge, Georgia, plant, Levi Strauss told the hourly workers, "You are the experts. If you meet predetermined production goals and predetermined absenteeism and safety standards, we'll split 50-50 with you any savings that result from economies or productivity improvements."

"Sewing-machine operators," said CEO Robert Haas, "are now running the plant. They're making the rules and in some cases changing them, because they understand why the rules are there and which rules make sense and which don't. They're taking initiatives and making things work better because it's in their interest, and they don't have to be told."[5]

Educating Managers and Supervisors

The team system changes the roles of managers and supervisors. The manager no longer gives orders but provides support and counsel.

Sometimes, managers and supervisors have problems adjusting to these new roles. Robert Frey recalls the attitude of Cin-Made managers when he sought to empower his employees.

Frey launched his cultural change by making two pronouncements:

- I do not choose to own a company that has an adversarial relationship with its employees.
- Employee participation will play an essential role in management.

"To my surprise, the very act of making these two statements seemed to increase the level of adversarial behavior," Frey recalled. "First of all, my three managers felt they were paid to be worthy adversaries of the [workers]. It's what they'd been trained for. It's what made them good managers. Moreover, they were not used to participation in any form, certainly not in decision making. One of them devised at least a dozen ways of delaying and obstructing the flow of necessary numbers to the employees. As for profit sharing, another of my managers declared it to be a form of communism. They all saw both of my statements as clear threats to their positions."[6]

Larger companies, too, must re-educate their managers and supervisors in their new roles. Levi Strauss learned this when it inaugurated its cultural change.

"There's a whole range of behaviors that were highly functional in the old hierarchical organization that are dead wrong in the flatter, more responsive, empowered organization that we're seeking to become," said Haas.[7]

To inculcate these values in its supervisory staff, Levi Strauss codified its values in an "Aspirations Statement." This statement was to provide a guideline for decisions and behavior throughout the corporation. The company then put its top 700 people through a "Leadership Week." This was a course designed to educate managers in the behavior mandated by the Aspirations Statement. Twenty managers per week took the course until all 700 had completed it.

LEADERS CAN BECOME DOWNERS

Leadership courses can teach your managers and supervisors to work with your employees instead of ruling over them.

I've spent a lot of time observing and studying human behavior in the work place, and I've noted that managers and supervisors can assume roles that cast them as either *downers* or *lifters*.

Here are some roles DOWNERS play:

D odos

O bfuscators

W imps

N aggers

E xecutioners

R oad hogs

S ocial directors

DODOS

You've heard of dodos. They're extinct birds. The reason they're extinct is that they were sluggish and slow to adapt to the times. When their environment changed, they went on behaving in the old ways. Today's management dodos are likewise wedded to the old ways. They look with suspicion on any new ideas. If it hasn't been done before, they don't want to try it now. People who work for dodos never learn new things because dodos are convinced that nothing new is worthwhile. Companies that are over-populated with dodos are on their way to extinction.

OBFUSCATORS

Obfuscator is a $40 word for a person who makes things as murky and unclear as possible. These managers try to hide from responsibility in fogs of confusion. Their motto is, "When you figure out what I want, I'll let you know." They keep their people in the dark about where they're trying to lead them and what's expected of each member of the team.

People who work for obfuscators spend a lot of time trying to figure out what the boss wants and not enough time adding value to the company's products and services.

WIMPS

Wimps hate everybody, but wouldn't dare tell people to their faces.

They abhor conflict, so they're afraid to confront people — at least directly. A wimp may go behind the backs of employees and criticize them before others, hoping the third party will do their dirty work for them. But often, unproductive behavior goes unchallenged, the wimp's department drifts along without strong leadership, and the people who work for it have a low regard for the company, its leaders and themselves.

NAGGERS

Naggers are never satisfied. If their people achieve excellence, they demand perfection. Whatever their people do is not good enough. If you were to give them a free pass through the Pearly Gates, they'd complain about the glare from the streets of gold and would swear that the angelic choir sang off key. Actually, they're the ones off key, and their carping is devastating to staff morale.

EXECUTIONERS

Executioners always seem ready to drop the guillotine on somebody's neck. They use fear as a motivational tool. Their motto is "Go ahead — make my day!" Their idea of inspiring their staffs to action is to say "Do it or get fired."

Around executioners, people are afraid to think, so they do exactly as they're told and secretly hope it makes the boss look foolish.

ROAD HOGS

Road hogs don't believe in sharing the road or sharing the action. Their premise is that if you want something done right, you have to do it yourself. They're afraid to empower people because they see two possible consequences:

1. The people they empower will succeed, and thus take the glory and the reward away from the road hog.
2. The people they empower will fail, and the road hog will be saddled with the blame.

As a result, they're the only people in their organizations who are authorized to think and to act, so the operation becomes starved for new ideas.

SOCIAL DIRECTORS

These friendly, cheerful executives often ask, "Is everybody happy?" If everybody isn't happy, social directors take full responsibility. To these generous souls, everybody's problems are their problems, and they try to solve them all.

As a result, they end up with staffers who can't solve problems for themselves. Generously shouldering everyone's problems, social directors soon find themselves enmeshed in a tangle of other people's problems and are unable to get their own jobs done.

. . . OR THEY CAN BECOME LIFTERS

These supervisors and managers need to overhaul their attitudes and transform themselves into *lifters*.

Here are some roles *lifters* play:

L iberators

I nspirers

F acilitators

T eachers

E mpowerers

R ole models

S moothers

LIBERATORS

Managers and supervisors who step into the liberator's role free their people to engage in creative, innovative thinking. They expect people to try new things and to fail at many of them. They even reward constructive failures.

How can a failure be constructive?

A failure is constructive when it yields knowledge and insights leading to ultimate successes. If it adds to the collective knowledge of the organization, it is constructive.

A study of more than 150 new products concluded that "the knowledge gained from failures [is] often instrumental in achieving subsequent successes. In the simplest terms, failure is the ultimate teacher.[8]

Liberators also make it possible for their employees to come to them with the bad news, realizing that what they don't know can hurt them. Along with Patrick Henry, they say, ". . . Whatever anguish of spirit it may cost, I am willing to know the whole truth; to know the worst, and to provide for it."

INSPIRERS

Inspirers show people exciting possibilities and encourage them to aim for them. They help people acquire confidence and optimism.

The role of the inspirer calls for enthusiasm. Inspirers know that leaders must be excited about their jobs if they expect the people around them to be excited.

Inspirers know that nothing fuels the fires of enthusiasm like genuine praise. Managers and supervisors who play this role like to catch people doing something right and commend them for it. Inspirers give compliments in public, criticism in private. They highlight people's potential instead of their failures, and they reward progress.

FACILITATORS

Facilitators make it easy for people to do their jobs. They guide the efforts of employees toward common objectives.

Facilitators step confidently into the roles of problem-solvers. They're like skilled loggers looking for the one log that will unlock the logjam that prevents the timber from floating downstream. Facilitators help the people around them locate and remove the "key logs" when problems block the stream of progress in the organization.

Facilitators also practice good communication. This means speaking and writing so that they are understood, and listening so that they understand others.

Facilitators let their people know how they work. They don't assume that being the boss automatically means that people know you. Facilitators let people know when it's all right to interrupt them with non-emergency issues, when to leave them undisturbed except for emergencies, and what tack to take in bringing problems to the facilitator's attention.

Facilitators make it known that they want and welcome the input and feedback of those under their supervision.

TEACHERS

Teachers help others to learn how and why, not just what. They are not content to provide their employees with mere training in tasks and procedures. They educate them to find their own solutions to problems, and empower them to act on their solutions.

Teachers make clear what is expected of their subordinates, and follow up to see whether the expectations are being met. Then they give positive feedback, praising the good performance, identifying areas in need of improvement, and helping people find ways to improve.

EMPOWERERS

Empowerers help people discover better ways of doing things. They don't feel the need to do everything themselves. Like Bear Bryant, the great University of Alabama football coach, they believe in sharing the glory and hogging the blame. The Bear once said:

If anything goes bad, then I did it. If anything goes semi-good, then we did it. If anything goes real good, then you did it. That's all it takes to get people to win football games for you.

Under Bear Bryant, the Crimson Tide won a lot of football games.

ROLE MODELS

Good leaders must become what they want their followers to become. They guide by example. You don't acquire leadership ability through appointment. You acquire it by winning the support and commitment of the people around you to reach the common goals of your company.

SMOOTHERS

Smoothers are the diplomats in the organization. When they see conflict, they find ways to resolve it. The look for ways to achieve cooperation instead of competition among team members. They help people maintain cooperative relationships with their peers and with other levels of management.

EDUCATING FOR THE CORE QUALITIES

Good leaders at one time or another must assume each of these positive roles. The ability to step into these roles requires certain inner characteristics that can also be learned.

The core qualities are these:

- *Teachability*. The modern organization must constantly acquire new knowledge and new expertise. That means its leaders must be open to new ideas and methods. They must be able to listen, observe and learn.

- *Adaptability*. Today's business organizations stand or fall on the basis of their ability to ride the tiger of change. This requires leaders who are willing and able to adjust to fast-changing technology, market conditions and social conditions.

- *Flexibility*. Today's American work force is the most diverse in history. The United States is a kaleidoscope of ethnic and cultural groups, and the work force reflects that diversity. Those who would lead these workers must be able to deal smoothly and tactfully with people of different cultural and ethnic backgrounds; with different temperaments and behavior styles.

- *Creativity*. Leaders must be willing to take innovative chances and encourage those around them to do the same.

- *Sensitivity*. They must be conscious of the feelings, needs and desires of others.

EDUCATING EMPLOYEES FOR NEW ROLES

If management desires to turn its employees into partners, it must educate them to shoulder their new responsibilities.

The workers must understand their new roles. They must be taught to shed their worker mentalities and cultivate the mentality of entrepreneurs.

Assuming these responsibilities requires that workers develop these key attributes:

- The technical competence to do their jobs.
- Human-relations skills.
- A feeling that what they do is meaningful.
- A sense of influence within the organization.

Without technical competence, the job doesn't get done, so that's a minimum requirement for any job. That's where training is valuable.

Without human-relations skills, a worker impedes instead of advancing team effort. In the modern work place, people have to be able to get along. That's where education is valuable.

EDUCATING IN CONFLICT RESOLUTION

Getting along becomes easier when the work force enjoys effective communication skills. The ability to make known your wants and needs assertively but tactfully is a powerful work-place asset. It enables people to respect the needs of others without sacrificing their own interests.

No work place, however, will be entirely free of conflict. If people are to be taught to work together in teams, they must also be taught how to resolve the inevitable differences. So an education in conflict resolution is essential to a productive work force.

This is the one area where the old-style supervisor will most often be missed. In the old hierarchical environment, a supervisor could quickly put a lid on a dispute by rendering an arbitrary decision. In the team setting, workers may rarely see bosses, so disputes can simmer until they flare.

Part of management's challenge is to determine at what point the workers in a group have achieved the level of maturity necessary to make teamwork practical. Sometimes, it's necessary to abolish the team and reinstate formal supervision until that level has been achieved.

But it's also possible to teach workers how to get the dispute off the floor and into a conference room. Often, the team leader or a seasoned worker who enjoys the respect of teammates, can step in as a mediator. A good educational process can equip your employees to handle most such disputes on their own.

PUTTING MEANING INTO THE JOB

But as we have seen, technical skills and behavioral skills provide only the foundation for a good, productive work force. Unless the job's meaning for the worker goes deeper than the physical or rote tasks it requires, the worker won't be truly happy and won't achieve optimum productivity.

Philosopher Abraham Maslow is famous for his "hierarchy of human needs." He portrayed these needs in a pyramid, rising from the primitive needs of food, clothing and shelter up through the higher needs of social belonging, self-esteem and self-actualization — becoming all that you can be.

Most Americans have moved into the middle to upper levels of Maslow's pyramid. Most jobs provide the necessities of life and then some. People now are working to satisfy their higher values: a sense of belonging to a larger group, a feeling of accomplishment, and a sense of becoming all that they can be. They need to know that they are accomplishing something significant. They need to identify with the company, feeling its success as their success.

If your workers' jobs are to be meaningful for them, they must be interested in more than the performance of mechanical and rote functions. They must be taught to make decisions for themselves. If your business is a thinking organism, workers can't look to management for the answers to every problem.

LETTING EMPLOYEES MAKE THEIR OWN DECISIONS

Johnsonville Foods of Sheboygan, Wisconsin, was a pioneer in the practice of participative management. CEO Ralph Stayer followed the premise that employees ought to solve the problems that relate to the work place.

When some of his people complained about fellow employees who played their boom boxes too loud, Stayer refused to referee the dispute. He told his employees to solve the situation any way they wished.

When they complained about the vending machines in the company cafeteria, he told them, "I don't eat at the vending machines; get whatever company you want."

If you're the CEO, says Stayer, "You don't make the decision. Your job is to transfer the ownership of the problem to where it belongs."[9]

Decision-making is risky. The person who makes the decision becomes accountable for the results of the decision. Therefore, companies who expect their employees to take over decision-making responsibility must educate them in effective decision-making and risk-taking.

Employees need to learn what kind of information they need to make decisions and how to obtain it.

TRUSTING EMPLOYEES WHEN THEY'RE WRONG

Employees, of course, will sometimes make the wrong decisions. This shouldn't surprise you. Have all your decisions been the correct ones? Some of mine have been lulus, and I'll bet you're still cringing over some of yours.

So management must be willing to trust employees to make the *wrong* decisions, and to back them up when they do. Some companies make a big deal of "empowering" their employees. They encourage independent decision-making, but the first time an employee throws away the book and bases a decision on a real-life situation involving a real-life customer, management gets cold feet.

But that's precisely where participative management can make a positive difference. Employees who are not bound by the inflexible rules found in policy manuals can make decisions based on the best interests of the company and the customer in *that particular situation.* A good educational program will equip your employees to make such decisions confidently, and in the long-term interests of the company. A good educational process also will help management cultivate confidence in the employees at the same time employees acquire confidence in themselves. If one gets there before the other, you'll have problems.

SEVEN PRINCIPLES OF EFFECTIVE MANAGEMENT

The secret to turning your employees into partners can be summed up in seven principles of management that can be achieved through an integrated educational approach:

1. MANAGE PEOPLE, NOT JUST PRODUCTION.

The machinery tends to function smoothly when the people who run it function smoothly. You can have the finest buildings equipped with the latest in state-of-the-art equipment. But if your employees are disgruntled, passive, unskilled, undereducated and motivated in conflicting directions, your physical resources will not bring you good performance, productivity or profitability.

2. INSPIRE PEOPLE, DON'T JUST DRIVE THEM.

You can inspire people by showing them how to be their very best.

Executives can inspire employees by giving them a cause to rally behind: an inspiring corporate vision and mission based on values the employees can identify with.

3. BE EASY TO RESPECT AND LOOK UP TO.

You don't gain respect by sitting in an ivory tower and looking down on the work floor. Be accessible to employees and let them see your human side.

Employees are turned off by supervisors, managers, and executives who pretend to be infallible. Observe high standards of personal conduct, but let your employees know that you're human. Talk to them about your bad decisions as well as your good ones. When you blow it, grin and admit it. Your employees will respect you for it.

4. BE EASY TO LIKE AND GET ALONG WITH.

Once, on a televised tour of a plant, Remington CEO Victor Kiam stepped off-camera to ask a woman employee about her ailing husband. He told her not to try to carry the burden alone. The company was there to help. Later, the woman told an observer that she would do anything for Kiam.

That kind of loyalty isn't earned by prickly, aloof executives. Kiam obviously had taken the time to mingle with employees and talk to them about their problems.

5. HELP PEOPLE LIKE THEMSELVES.

Robert W. Reasoner, a California school superintendent, who headed a statewide task force on self-esteem, identified five basic attitudes that foster self-esteem. They are a sense of security, a sense of identity, a sense of belonging, a sense of purpose, and a sense of personal competence.

Secure people are comfortable with who they are and with what others think about them. They know their roles in the organization and are confident that they can fill them.

People with a sense of identity know how they fit into the work place and how the work place fits into their lives. To them, work takes its place among family, friends and community as an important and fulfilling component of their lives.

When your employees have a sense of belonging, they identify with the company's vision and goals, because these things have personal meaning for them. They personally share in the success and the prestige of the company.

Employees obtain a sense of purpose from knowing the company's goals and knowing how their efforts contribute toward those goals. Management must take employees into its confidence and give them a role in planning and goal-setting.

You can give your employees a sense of personal competence by educating them for their jobs and giving them the freedom to succeed or fail on their own.

6. HELP PEOPLE BELIEVE THAT WHAT THEY'RE DOING IS IMPORTANT.

Medtronic, Inc., of Minneapolis has a heart-warming way of dramatizing the importance of what its employees do. Each year at Christmas time, the company holds a party for employees. Guests of honor are people whose lives have been prolonged by Medtronic cardio-pulmonary devices.

Stew Leonard, the grocery-store wizard from Connecticut, told me he refuses to use job titles that he perceives as demeaning. Once he noticed a job listed as "popcorn maker." He immediately ordered a more dignified title. How would you feel if someone asked you what you did for a living and you had to answer, "I'm a popcorn maker"?

7. BE RESPONSIVE TO PEOPLE. LISTEN TO PEOPLE. READ PEOPLE. RESPOND; DON'T REACT.

Leaders should be accessible to the people they lead. Let your employees know they can come to you with problems, concerns, ideas, suggestions or complaints. If they bring usable ideas, adopt the ideas and give the employees credit.

Welcome bad news as well as the good. Don't ignore complaints. Listen to them. Find out what you can do to rectify matters, let the employees know what you plan to do — and do it.

To make these principles a part of everyday life in your company, you must give your human-resources staff the go-ahead and the necessary tools to educate your people toward a partnership mind-set. Mind-sets, by definition, are inner qualities that must be instilled through education, not installed through training.

Your employees become your partners when they buy into your corporate vision, values and mission. They become deeply committed when they create personal visions that are congruent with the corporate vision. Your corporate education system can be a pillar of support for this congruence. The next chapter will explain how.

CHAPTER SIX

PILLAR FOUR: EDUCATING FOR CONGRUENCE

Your work force consists of a wide range of individuals with a wide variety of dreams. People tend to exert their best efforts when their efforts are carrying them toward their dreams. Therefore, your employees will contribute more to your company if they can fulfill their dreams while working toward company goals.

As we learned in Chapter Five, to chart a course toward the future it desires, your organization creates a corporate vision and drafts a mission statement.

Individuals must create personal visions if they are to fulfill their dreams of personal success. To make their maximum contributions toward corporate success, those personal visions should harmonize with your corporate vision. This convergence of personal and corporate visions is what we mean by *congruence*.

PEOPLE WITHOUT VISIONS, VALUES AND GOALS

Most people go through life without well-thought-out goals based on clear values and strong visions. They take whatever opportunities come along, wandering down whatever roads open up for them, and then wonder why none of these roads lead to success.

These are the people who come to work and do their jobs without giving much thought to the way their jobs fit into the corporate picture or how their efforts might promote the corporate welfare.

If you can teach these people to create personal visions that dovetail with the corporate vision and to set personal goals in harmony with corporate goals, you can channel a tremendous surge of energy into the advancement of corporate interests.

PEOPLE SEEKING SELF-FULFILLMENT

For others — especially those of the younger generation — it isn't enough that a job offer steady work and steady pay. For them, it has to be meaningful as well. They want to feel that they're becoming all that they can be. This is the self-actualization tier of Abraham Maslow's hierarchy of human needs.

People who feel this way may look upon jobs as simply means to an end — the end being ultimate self-fulfillment. Such people will feel no loyalty to a company that does not offer them this avenue to the top of the Maslow pyramid.

For these people, management's challenge is to help them see how the fulfillment of corporate objectives will help them achieve personal fulfillment. When the personal vision has been brought into alignment with the corporate vision, then a powerful synergy develops.

FOCUSING THROUGH
YOUR CORPORATE VISION

When you have a work force full of people who have made the corporate vision a part of their personal visions, you have an energized work force.

How do you accomplish this?

Basically, you have to make your corporate vision the instrument for focusing other visions throughout your organization.

If your company consists of several business units, each unit should have a vision that supports the corporate vision. Each department should have a vision that supports the business unit's vision. Each team should have a vision that supports the departmental vision. And each team member should have a personal vision that harmonizes with the visions of the team, department, business-unit and corporation.

BUILDING ON VALUES

If the corporate vision is to serve as a focusing instrument for smaller-scale visions within the company, it has to be based on an inspiring set of values that people in all areas of the company can easily embrace and adopt as their own. These values can be identified through a process that involves people at every level of the company. In Chapter Five, we learned how Duke Power Company accomplished this. Such broad-based participation makes it easier for employees to create personal visions in harmony with the corporate vision.

ORGANIZATIONAL AND PERSONAL FOCUS

Your company cannot create an effective corporate vision unless it achieves organizational focus. Your employees cannot create effective personal visions unless they have been taught to achieve personal focus.

Therefore, your educational process should include courses that help people arrive at personal focus and that help management lead in achieving organizational focus.

To achieve organizational focus, executives must make known the company's vision, mission, values and goals. They must then show how the efforts of the employees contribute toward achievement of these.

This calls for intelligent communication at many levels. All the company's communication tools should be used in a coordinated effort to make the company's vision come alive to employees. Executive speeches to employees should emphasize the vision. Company publications should make the vision a continuing theme. Bulletin boards should reflect the vision and its supporting mission and goals. The vision should shine through the annual report. The vision statement should be on the tip of every tongue in the organization.

IDENTIFYING CORPORATE VALUES

The corporate vision can be created and the corporate mission articulated only after the company has identified its corporate values.

We've found that when individuals and organizations take the time to identify the qualities they value, the lists of personal and organizational values correspond rather closely. Each list usually contains such values as honesty, integrity, service to others, creativity, profitability or financial security, open communication, and fun.

One of my corporate clients has adopted a mission statement that reflects these values:

- Providing top-quality products and services fairly priced to our customers.
- Employing and developing high-achieving people, and
- Providing them with the education and supervision they need to realize their full potential.
- Recognizing and rewarding high performance.

- Encouraging teamwork.
- Expecting loyalty and commitment.
- Achieving quality and consistently increasing earnings.
- Being a good corporate citizen in the communities we serve by encouraging our people to be involved in community development and providing financial support to quality community needs.
- Participating in mergers that are beneficial to long-range shareholder wealth.
- Building market share and increasing volumes per capital and operating funds deployed.
- Conducting all aspects of our business within the highest ethical standards.

These are values the vast majority of its employees could easily embrace. They could serve as the foundation for personal visions and for organizational visions at the team, departmental and corporate levels.

STEPS TOWARD A VISION

The vision represents the individual's and company's desired future, based on the values.

Before a company creates its vision, however, it must take an intensive and intelligent look at itself, its employees, its resources and its market in the light of its values.

Here are some steps we recommend to our clients:

- Identify your unique position in the market-place: Decide what you do better than anybody else.

- Identify the type of customers you want, what needs they have, and ways you can effectively meet those needs.

- Focus your market: Identify your potential customers, and divide them into segments that can be readily identified by specific needs. Decide which ones you need to serve and what resources you'll have to commit.

- Identify the products you now offer, their features, their end uses, and their technical components.

- Identify the products you'll *need* to offer to serve the customers you want to serve.

- Identify the resources you'll need to serve your chosen market.

- Identify your current and potential competitors, their costs, their prices, their delivery systems, their assets and their locations.

- Analyze the risks involved in serving your market.

After examining all those factors, look 15 to 20 years down the road and determine what your company should be like at that time. Who would its customers be? What would be its strengths? How many branches would it have? What would its profit-and-loss statement look like?

When you've made these determinations, you'll be in a better position to create a vision and rally the work force behind it.

Next, we suggest that division or department heads perform the same type of analysis on their individual departments. They might choose several areas that they consider vital to the functioning of their areas of responsibility. If anything were possible, how would they want their departments to look 10 years down the road?

CREATING THE PERSONAL VISION

To create a personal vision, individuals need to take a similarly intensive look at themselves. This type of personal examination can help employees at all levels focus their personal identities and align their purposes with the corporate vision.

The personal vision, like the corporate vision, begins with values. Individuals need to list the values that mean most to them in their personal and professional lives. Then they can list the behaviors that support those values and those that conflict with them. These lists provide a foundation on which to build the personal vision.

To provide shape and form for the vision, the individual needs to achieve personal focus. A human life has many facets, and truly effective, well-rounded individuals need to focus each aspect. Here are some areas that need to be focused:

PERSONAL IDENTITY

Your personal identity is the sum total of who you are and why you are here. What contribution do you expect to make during your existence on this planet?

Personal identity may have many components. It may include one's role in the family, in religion, and in the community. These questions can help in pinpointing an individual's personal identity:

1. What do you value most?
2. What one thing do you worry about most?
3. What one thing do you talk about most?
4. Which of your talents have you developed most fully and relied on most often?
5. What kind of challenge do you find most appealing?
6. What one thing have you done in your life that you have been most proud of?
7. What one thing have you done in your life that you would most like to do differently? Or what have you not done that you wish you had done?
8. What are the three most important ingredients of your personal identity?
9. What do you do that other people often observe and appreciate?
10. If you discovered that you only had 90 days to live, what three things would you do?

A company benefits when its work force consists of people who have stable families, solid moral and ethical standards, and active interests in their communities, their schools and the other institutions that hold communities together.

To encourage such values, the company as a corporate entity must set the proper example. If it wants employees to follow high ethical standards, it too must observe high ethical standards. If it wants employees who are involved in community activities, it must itself become involved in such activities. If it wants employees who respect the natural environment, it must take care that its own actions show such respect.

The company's mission and the personal missions of its employees can thus become mutually reinforcing.

YOUR PROFESSIONAL PURPOSE

The most critical ingredient of success in any venture is a clear picture of what you are trying to achieve. If an employee's purpose is to "fill whatever capacity the company asks me to fill," then the employee is professionally unfocused.

Regardless of what field you're in, there has to be a professional *raison d'etre*: a reason for being what you are. Focused individuals seek to fill needs that cannot be met by people without their specific qualities and talents. So each of your employees needs to ask: "What are the specific needs I propose to fill, and how do I propose to fill them?"

Individuals can focus their professional purposes by answering these questions:

1. What is the guiding or controlling idea in my life?
2. What is my strategy for implementing that idea?
3. What are my three greatest strengths and what am I doing to capitalize on them?
4. What are my three greatest weaknesses, and what am I doing to compensate for them?

Real winners seem to get life sorted out; they know where they are going and what they are doing.

YOUR PROFESSIONAL SELF-IMAGE

How you develop your professional career depends upon how you envision your role in that career. You can look at your career role as either a worker or as an entrepreneur. You don't have to be an hourly employee to have a worker mentality. And you don't have to be an independent businessperson to have an entrepreneurial mentality. What we're talking about here are basic attitudes and not occupational categories.

Those who follow the worker mentality do not discern a clear connection between their own success and the success of the company. They are not overly concerned about the company's marginal performance so long as they continue to draw paychecks and receive their annual increases. They may attend to their own areas competently, but will not worry greatly about what happens outside their areas of responsibility.

Those who follow the entrepreneurial mentality see themselves as partners in prosperity with the company. They view the company's ups and downs as *their* ups and downs, and are constantly looking for things that they personally can do to contribute to the company's profitability. They see the company as a boundaryless institution, and look for ways that they can make a difference in all aspects of its operations.

Workers accept a ceiling on success in return for a steady income. They are not boat-rockers, but believe in doing things the way they've always been done — which they perceive as the safe, cautious way.

Entrepreneurs are willing to take intelligent risks, accepting the possibility of failure as a fair price for the opportunity to grow.

Workers concentrate on the means. They do their jobs without worrying about how their jobs contribute to the total picture.

Entrepreneurs concentrate on the ends. They see their jobs in terms of how they contribute to the company's success.

The new business environment places a premium on the entrepreneurial mentality. Your company needs people who see themselves not just as beneficiaries of the company's success but as contributors to it.

Your employees can focus their career self-images by deciding what roles they want to play in the company's success, then forming mental pictures of themselves in those roles. These questions can help an employee focus on the desired role:

- How does what you do all day square with the way you see yourself? How does it square with the way you want to be seen by your coworkers?

- What is the most vital role you play in your company?

- What are your secondary roles and what percentage of your time is spent on each?

- Which two of your present roles would you rather not be playing?

- Which roles would you rather be playing instead?

- What is your career mission and how will you know when you are accomplishing it?

To create their personal visions, employees must get in touch with their higher values. They must ask: "If anything were possible, what would I want to be?" The answer has to be something that is ambitious, yet achievable.

The vision can be built around answers to these three questions:

1. What are the attributes and abilities that set me apart from other people?
2. In what ways do I make use of these attributes and abilities?
3. If I could have everything the way I wanted it, what would my world look like? How would conditions differ from present conditions? How would it feel to live and work in such a world?

A personal vision is an individual's mental picture of the desired future. That mental picture sets up a creative tension that tends to draw the individual toward fulfillment of the vision. The vision can simplify decision-making, because all a person needs to ask about an option under consideration is "Does it harmonize with or support my vision?"

Once individuals have created their personal visions, they have to commit themselves to the fulfillment of the visions. They must learn to set long-range, medium-range and short-range goals leading toward their desired futures. Then they have to create action plans to carry them toward those goals.

BENEFITS OF PERSONAL VISIONS

Personal visions can focus your employees' thoughts and actions in powerful ways. Here are some of the benefits:

- Employees can constantly redirect their time, energy, talents, expertise, and money from areas of low yield or no yield to areas of high yield.
- They can systematically develop their most productive strengths and compensate for their most costly weaknesses.
- They can qualify the results they expect and measure their performance hourly, daily, weekly and annually.
- They can identify obstacles and problems and attack them effectively.
- They can identify the most productive ideas and go after the greatest opportunities.
- They can communicate clearly and persuasively with people who can help them achieve their goals.
- They can become competent enough at what they do to approach every opportunity with complete confidence.
- They can have more fun at everything they do.

CONGRUENCE LEADS TO SUCCESS

When your employees have been involved in the creation of corporate, departmental and team visions, these visions can become part of their everyday behavior. When they can buy into the company's values, the corporate values can be incorporated into their personal values. These personal values in turn form the basis for their personal visions. Personal goals are set in harmony with team, departmental and corporate goals. The employee is now pulling in the same direction as the team, the department and the company. When your whole work force is working toward personal visions aligned with corporate visions, the congruence becomes a powerful force for corporate success.

THE TASK OF EDUCATION

Your employees will not create their personal visions spontaneously. To achieve the desired congruence between individual visions and corporate visions, your educational process must accomplish these things:

- Introduce your employees to the concept of visioning.
- Demonstrate to them the effectiveness of visioning.
- Promote corporate-wide awareness of corporate values and the corporate vision.
- Teach them how to identify personal values.
- Teach them how to create personal visions.
- Demonstrate to them the rewards that follow from achieving congruence between personal and corporate visions.

A LONG-TERM PROCESS

This is not a quick fix. Achieving congruence is a long-term, never-ending process. Once you've made the one-time change to a corporate culture that stresses employee involvement, your job is not finished. New people are constantly joining the work force, and they too must be absorbed into the culture; they too must achieve congruence with the corporate vision.

In some respects, participative management complicates recruiting and hiring. When the team system is working well, the teams are more than work groups; they're social groups as well. The new hire must join an existing team whose members already have worked out the personal and procedural relationships that lead to optimum performance. The newcomer's unfamiliarity with the system may, at first, dampen team performance.

But educational processes can be designed to speed up the new hire's social and occupational transition. The newcomer's orientation should include thorough instruction in the company's vision, values and goals as well as any needed training in rules, procedures and mechanical processes. Newcomers can be helped to form their own personal visions in harmony with team and corporate visions.

Best results are often obtained when the teams themselves participate in the selection of personnel. They can then look for the qualities that will support their team's vision. A "buddy system" may be developed to allow older hands to work with newcomers until the newcomers have bonded with the team. The buddy system will be more effective when the older hands have been well grounded in communication skills, behavior styles and principles of participative management. This too is a task for your education and development department.

It should be obvious that congruence can never be achieved without an educational process that supports the corporate vision. People must be taught to identify their values, create their visions, set goals, and devise and execute action plans. They must know the corporate vision and the values on which it is based. And they must cultivate the attitudes that move them to incorporate the corporate vision into their own personal visions.

This educational process can infuse your company with energy in a way that training alone cannot match. When your human-resource people are empowered to add education to their training mission, that energy is directed toward goals of quality and excellence. It can then propel your company to new heights of success. In Chapter Seven, we will describe the educational pillar that supports the continuous-improvement process — the process necessary to achieving and sustaining quality and excellence.

CHAPTER SEVEN

PILLAR FIVE:
EDUCATING FOR QUALITY

In American business, quality used to be controlled by inspecting the end product and either fixing the defects or throwing the defective unit into the scrap heap.

Those were the bad old days when American products were taking a sound beating in the global marketplace and the "Made in USA" label was in danger of becoming a badge of second-rate quality.

American products began to regain their luster when business leaders started to adopt the principle that you have to build quality in instead of inspecting defects out.

To build quality in required an entirely new mind-set among management and employees.

Over the last few years, I have watched admiringly as many of my consulting clients have, one by one, taken significant steps to install quality-assurance programs. Such companies as INA Bearing, Bama Foods, Southern National and the Rives companies have made significant improvements in productivity and have developed ways to serve their customers better through cultivating a quality mindset among their people.

One of the first things that had to change was the definition of quality. Quality not only means "free of defects," but also — in the definition applied by the Xerox Corporation — "fully meeting customer requirements."

This definition can be applied in both the manufacturing and the service sectors. It requires much more than basic job skills. To produce true quality, as defined by the customers, a corporation must know the customers' needs and must look for innovative ways to meet those needs.

EDUCATING FOR
CONTINUOUS IMPROVEMENT

To return quality to American products, businesses have embarked on a variety of programs under the name of "Total Quality Management."

The name suggests that "total quality" is a goal that can be attained and, once attained, can be maintained.

But if quality is defined by customer needs, then "total quality" can never be a fixed target, because customer needs constantly change.

For this reason, many management specialists are describing the quality-enhancement processes as "continuous improvement."

Whatever it's called and however companies will address the issues specifically in the future, one thing is certain: Customers *expect* quality, and companies that don't provide it won't have many customers. In one form or another, the quality movement is here to stay.

EDUCATION AT THE ORGANIZATIONAL LEVEL

The achievement of true customer-satisfying quality calls for education at the organizational level.

Charles R. Lee, chairman and CEO of the GTE Corporation, has stressed the importance of education in his company's continuous improvement process.

"Many businesses have adopted total quality programs and implemented quality training for individuals or small teams," he noted, but "few have taken the next step . . . elevating learning to the organizational level."

In implementing the process, said Lee, "Our first step, and by far the most important one, was to develop an educational program that would reach all levels of our employees. To date, we have taught total quality courses to over 10,000 employees."[1]

Xerox also put the emphasis on company-wide education when it embarked on its "Leadership

Through Quality" initiative. Xerox invested $125 million and more than 4 million employee hours over a four-year period to provide its employees with quality-related education. The resurgence of the formerly ailing giant to vibrant corporate health proves the wisdom of the investment.

CULTURE CHANGE IS MANDATORY

Education in quality requires more than the acquisition of mechanical skills and training in histograms, the Pareto principle and statistical process analysis — although such training plays an important role in the delivery of quality.

The key to building quality into your organizational processes is to help your people — from top to bottom — cultivate an attitude of excellence, and to make it a part of their everyday activities.

Some companies drill their employees in the techniques of statistical process control and declare that to be "total quality management," said Bob Joines, vice president at Eastman Chemical, a 1993 winner of the federal government's Baldridge Award for quality. "To do it right, you have to change your culture as much as your processes."[2]

One of the most frequent causes of the failure of Total Quality Management initiatives is the absence of a supportive culture. You cannot implement a program of continuous improvement until you have educated your employees in the attitudes and behaviors that produce continuous improvement. You cannot introduce such educational efforts in piecemeal fashion. The quality culture must pervade your organization.

THREE FUNDAMENTAL PRINCIPLES

The Federal Quality Institute has established three fundamental principles for building quality in:

1. Customer satisfaction.

2. Continuous improvement.

3. Responsibility on the part of each individual involved in producing products and services.

The third principle, in particular, requires a work force educated to pursue quality.

Here are some of the areas in which management and employees need to be educated if the company expects to excel in quality:

- *Communication.* Quality enhancement requires both the acquisition and the sharing of knowledge. This calls for skills in listening and reading as well as in speaking and writing. If people are unable to receive and send information clearly and accurately, they will be unable to share it throughout the organization, and quality will suffer.

- *Teamwork.* If quality is to be built in, then the focus must be on the process and not on the product. Since the process involves everyone, then everyone must be involved in quality. A process does not consist of a sequence of non-related activities. Each activity is related to the one downstream from it and the one upstream from it. Therefore, if true quality is to be achieved, everyone involved in the process must know what to do to meet the needs of the person downstream. This requires teamwork.

When Corning Inc., moved its molten metal filters operation into a new plant, it left it up to employees to determine how the machinery was to be arranged. They planned it so that team members could be within earshot of each other. By practicing teamwork principles, the workers were able to reduce flaws from 10,000 per million units in the old factory to three per million in the new one.

The work-flow arrangement at Corning made it easy for people to communicate and cooperate. In contrast, the old hierarchical environment encouraged internal competition instead of cooperation. In the old system, people were evaluated on individual efforts instead of team performance. This encouraged each person to try to outperform the other, because the worse others looked, the better you looked by comparison. As my friend, Charles Dygert, has often pointed out, "In cooperative situations, others are depending on you to succeed. In competitive situations, others hope to see you fail." So a quality-producing work force must be educated in team-building and team-based performance, where collaborative effort is the norm.

- *Involvement.* If everyone in your organization is to become involved in achievement of quality, it follows that everyone must have the authority to do something about quality. The Marriott Corporation, for instance, started calling its employees associates, and authorized them to make decisions on the spot without consulting their supervisors. They were given the green light to go beyond the policy manual and take any reasonable step to satisfy customers.

If involvement is to become a reality, all your managers and supervisors must know what to delegate, when to delegate, to whom to delegate, and how to delegate. The art of delegation is one of those "soft skills" that is vital to every quality effort.

- *Problem-Solving.* To achieve true quality control, your workers must learn to solve problems on their own. One of the first things they have to acquire is the ability to look at process instead of personalities. In a thinking organism, when something goes wrong, workers don't ask "Who did it?" They ask, "Why did it happen?" They look at the process, determine where the malfunction occurred, and devise a plan for preventing a recurrence.

Problem-solving and decision-making thus become crucial attributes for a quality-oriented work force. Xerox concentrated a great deal of educational energy on teaching its employees the six-step problem-solving model detailed in figure 7-1.

- *Feedback.* Employees need to know how well they are doing and in what areas they need to improve. The ability to offer constructive feedback is essential for managers, supervisors and team members in quality-oriented participative management. If individuals get no feedback, they get the impression that their performance is not important to you.

Step					
1. Identify and select the problem	**2.** Analyze the problem	**3.** Generate potential solutions	**4.** Select and plan solution	**5.** Implement the solution	**6.** Evaluate the solution
Question to be Answered					
What do we want to change?	What keeps us from reaching the desired state?	How could we make the change?	What's the best way to do it?	Are we following the plan?	How well did it work?
Expansion/Divergence					
Lots of problems for consideration	Lots of potential causes identified	Lots of ideas on how to solve the problem	Lots of criteria for evaluating potential solutions; lots of ideas on how to implement and evaluate selected solution		
Contraction/Convergence					
One problem statement; one desired state agreed upon	Key causes identified and verified	Potential solutions clarified	Criteria to use for evaluating solution agreed upon; implementation plans agreed upon	Implementation of agreed-on contingency plans (if necessary)	Effectiveness of solution agreed upon; continuing problems (if any) identified
What's needed to go to the next step					
Identification of the gap; desired state described in observable terms	Key causes documented and ranked	Solution list	Plan for making and monitoring the change; measurement criteria to evaluate solution's effectiveness	Solution in place	Verify that the problem is solved, or agreement to address continuing problems

Xerox's Problem-Solving Process

If they get only negative feedback, they become demoralized.

Effective feedback takes into consideration the environment in which an individual is working and how the individual's job relates to the team and to the corporate mission. It lets employees know what they are doing right and what changes they need to make to enhance their effectiveness.

Corporations that give managers and supervisors responsibility for evaluating and appraising employees without teaching them how to coach and counsel will get the kind of quality you get when you turn a bull loose in a china shop.

KNOWLEDGE FROM OUTSIDE THE ORGANIZATION

One of the most important steps in setting up a quality culture is elimination of the "NIH" syndrome. The initials stand for "not invented here." This mind-set can be deadly, because it isolates the company from the stream of innovative ideas flowing through its field. If you close your ears to what other companies are doing, you may find yourself blindsided by innovations that propel your competition toward success while leaving you dead in the water.

"All other things being equal," said Benjamin Disraeli, the 19th century British prime minister, "the person who succeeds will be the person with the best information."

And Frederick the Great of Prussia observed, "It is pardonable to be defeated, but never to be surprised."

To stay abreast of the competition, your employees need to be educated to look for usable information and ideas wherever they can find them.

BENEFITS FROM BENCHMARKING

One method of doing this is benchmarking. Many companies send their people on visits to other companies to find out what ideas are working for them. The other companies need not be companies in your own field. When Duke Power Company embarked on its quality initiative, it sent a middle-management team to companies such as Ford, Xerox and Honeywell — none of which was involved in the generation and sale of electric power. General Electric sent people to WalMart to learn what the retailing pacesetter was doing that could be of benefit to the equipment manufacturer.

XEROX AIMS FOR THE FUTURE

When Xerox embarked on its comeback, it wasn't satisfied to use the achievements of other companies as targets toward which to aim. It determined instead to observe what others were doing now, projecting what the best of them would be doing in the future, then matching those future standards, over and over.

As an indication of the importance of benchmarking, more than half the points on the scorecard for the Baldridge Award relate to comparisons between the company and its competitors.

BENCHMARKING CAVEATS

A word of caution: Benchmarking won't work unless you've first built that quality-oriented culture. Once the culture is in place, you're in position to take advantage of ideas from outside your company.

When you do undertake benchmarking, don't let it degenerate into tourism. Employees who have not been thoroughly educated in the quality culture may regard the benchmarking excursions as sightseeing expeditions in which they get the grand tour of the host company, say "Isn't that interesting?" then repair to the local golf courses, tennis courts or bistros.

KNOWING WHAT TO LOOK FOR

If you're going to achieve usable ideas, your employees need to know what to look for. They need to be educated in the standards by which customers judge the quality of your products and services.

Janet Myers, a colleague of mine who does a splendid job consulting with financial institutions across America, emphasizes six quality standards that apply both to products and to services.

They are:

- Performance
- Features
- Reliability

- Serviceability
- Aesthetics
- Perceived quality[3]

PERFORMANCE

Performance refers not only to how well your *products* perform but also to how well your *company* performs. What steps do you take to make sure that the product or service does all the things the customers expect it to do?

If you're in the banking industry, for instance, customers may evaluate your performance on the basis of how long they have to wait in line to make deposits, how long it takes to get a loan approved, or how quickly they can begin writing checks on a new account.

In the grocery business, it may come down to the length of lines at check-out counters. One grocery chain bolstered its performance in the customer's eyes by offering to take up to $25 off the grocery bills of customers who could not find a line with fewer than four shoppers ahead of them.

FEATURES

Features represent the "extras" that your products and services offer to customers. It's the chocolate mint on the pillow in the hotel room; the lighted vanity mirror in a luxury automobile; the easy-to-use tutorial in the software package. How useful and desirable are these features to the customers you are seeking? How easy are they to use?

RELIABILITY

A reliable product will give satisfactory performance day in and day out without a malfunction. Reliable service means meeting the needs of customers and clients day in and day out without foul-ups. It means airlines that get people — and their luggage — to and from their destinations on time. It means insurance policies that satisfy claims on time, with no surprises. It means delivery services that deliver goods to the right place at the right time — and in sound condition. It means restaurants that serve you the food you order prepared the way you ordered it and meeting the quality standards you expect. It means banks that handle customers' accounts without glitches.

SERVICEABILITY

Serviceability refers to the ease with which customers are able to make use of your product or service. Can a customer use the software you sell without first obtaining a master's degree in computer programming? Can a purchaser take your appliance home and immediately begin using it, without having to purchase auxiliary equipment and without having to go through an extensive learning program? When clients call your business with a problem, can they quickly reach the person who can help them with the problem?

AESTHETICS

People do judge books by their covers. If your business doesn't have a pleasant ambience, your clients and customers will perceive that as a quality defect. Noisy, smelly, unsightly, hot, or cold surroundings will turn off your customers. Poorly groomed employees who look unkempt and unprofessional will send your clientele out your front door in the direction of your competitors. Rundown buildings; poorly maintained parking lots, sidewalks and entry ways; and even untrimmed and unwatered shrubbery will reflect on the quality of your products and services.

This doesn't mean that mechanics have to dress like lawyers, or that plumbers have to be as spotless as surgeons. But even employees whose jobs require that they get their hands dirty can be conscientious about personal hygiene and personal grooming.

Employees whose jobs require that they deal directly with the public should be especially conscious of their aesthetic images. Secretaries, receptionists, salespeople, public-relations people and others who represent you before the public must know how to put their best foot forward — because their best foot is your company's best foot.

It isn't always easy to lay down hard-and-fast rules about dress and grooming, and some people are adept at looking slovenly even while observing all the codes. The most effective way to achieve quality in your corporate aesthetics is to make sure that your employees are conscious of the image you're trying to project and are taught the importance of appropriate dress and grooming.

PERCEIVED QUALITY

Perceived quality refers to any of the criteria by which customers are likely to judge your business. Does your company literature look tasteful and professional, or shoddy and cheap? Do your salespeople come across as helpful or as pushy? Is your company known for its participation in community life, or for its indifference? Are your people community leaders, or sideline bench-warmers?

EDUCATING YOUR EYES AND EARS

When employees are properly educated in all the aspects of quality, they can become your alert eyes and ears wherever they go. Whether they go down to the local WalMart to buy an extension cord or travel to Singapore on a benchmarking mission, they can bring back information that can help you in sustaining continuous quality improvement.

Benchmarking excursions should not be spur-of-the-moment undertakings. The people who study other operations should first identify the areas in which your company could best benefit from outside ideas. If you know what your problems are, you are in better position to recognize the solutions that others have found.

GE'S "QUICK RESPONSE" FROM DOWN UNDER

General Electric provides a good example of successful benchmarking. While speaking in Auckland one summer, I learned how GE found an appliance company in New Zealand that was using an innovative method of compressing product cycle times. It put the method through a trial run in a Canadian affiliate, then transferred it to its largest appliance complex in Louisville, Kentucky. The method, which GE dubbed "Quick Response," enabled the company to respond more quickly to customer needs and to reduce inventories by $200 million a year.

After introducing Quick Response in Louisville, GE brought people in from all 13 of its major businesses to study the method and adapt it to their own operations.

The people who spotted the method in New Zealand had to be familiar with General Electric's needs. Otherwise, they would not have spotted the connection between the New Zealanders' practices and GE's problems.

IDENTIFY COMPANIES YOU CAN LEARN FROM

Knowing your own problems isn't enough. To make your benchmarking tours something more than fishing expeditions, you need to identify the companies that have something to teach you. After identifying these companies, your people can make systematic site visits. These visits must be more than cursory walk-throughs. Your benchmarkers must conduct incisive interviews with knowledgeable people from the host company. They must know what questions to ask and how to ask them. If your people are not skilled in asking and listening, your benchmarking expedition will be a dry run.

SPREAD THE LEARNING

After acquiring this information, the benchmarkers must return to your company and share what they've learned. They must be able to give accurate descriptions of the practices they've observed and the results of those practices. They must be able to make intelligent recommendations based on their findings.

Obviously, benchmarkers must have technical expertise to understand the processes they're observing. But they need much broader skills if they are to serve as the eyes and ears for your organization and if they are to convert what they observe into practical, usable ideas. They must be able to pick up a piece of information here and an idea there, then relate all this intelligence to the specific needs of your company.

ASK YOUR CUSTOMERS

You don't always have to send high-level representatives on expensive tours of distant plants and exotic lands to pick up good benchmarking information. Your customers can tell you a great deal of what you need to know. They know their own needs, they generally know what the competition does to meet those needs, and they can provide you with a ready comparison of your performance with that of the competition.

USE YOUR SALESPEOPLE

Salespeople can be valuable contacts with your customers. Properly educated salespeople know how to ask customers about their experiences with your products and those of your competitors. They have their antennae out for new needs, new preferences and new competitive challenges. To bring you this information, they need solid sales training. But, equally important, they must be *educated* to see themselves as part of the company's overall quality effort.

TOP MANAGEMENT MEETS CUSTOMERS AND SHAREHOLDERS

Motorola's top management instituted a policy of meeting regularly with customers. These meetings helped Motorola's leaders stay abreast of customer needs and competitive challenges.

I serve on the board of directors of the Southern National Corporation, a $20 billion bank holding company with branches in over 200 cities in the Southeast. Its CEO, John Allison, has implemented many practices that keep his management team in close touch with shareholders. He is thus able to bolster the confidence of shareholders in his company and to receive from them helpful information about how the bank's services stand up to the competition.

One example which really impressed me was Allison's insistence on his management calling the top 200,000 customers of the bank when it merged with BB&T. They listened to customer concerns, answered questions, and nurtured loyalty. Incidentally, Allison ranks at the top of the list of executives who believe deeply in providing a solid, integrated educational program across all levels of his 9,000 employees.

MACHINE OPERATORS MEET CUSTOMERS

Sales and management people aren't the only ones who can learn from customers. Worthington Steel inaugurated a program that sent all its machine operators on periodic, unescorted trips to customers' factories to discuss their needs. These operators had to know the mechanical functions of their machinery — which means they had to receive good training. But to make these excursions helpful and productive, they needed skills far beyond those required to run the machines. These skills are instilled through education.

MILLIKEN'S "FIRST DELIVERY TEAMS"

Milliken, a textile company in the Carolinas, created "first-delivery teams" to accompany the first delivery of a product to a customer. These teams were taught to follow the Milliken product through the customer's production process to see how it was used. Then they were to develop ideas for further improvement.[4]

OTHER SOURCES OF OUTSIDE INFORMATION

TRADE SHOWS

Trade shows can also be valuable sources of information about what's going on inside your industry but outside your company. People who attend these shows can bring back the competition's literature and can gain insights into the latest preferences of customers and the latest advances among suppliers.

SUPPLIERS

Suppliers can tell you a great deal about where you stand with respect to your competitors. Chances are they're selling to your rivals as well as to you, and they may be able to pass on useful information without violating confidences.

DATABASES

Computerized databases can be rich sources of business intelligence. Some databases track corporate and scientific developments. Others contain information on specific industries. These high-tech bulletin boards are likely to proliferate in the future.

As of this writing, Knight-Ridder's Dialog has some 400 databases tracking corporate and scientific developments. McGraw Hill and Dun & Bradstreet maintain computer databases on specific industries. McGraw Hill's G. W. Dodge can provide information on the type of plant, size, lead contractors and other data that can be useful to you.

Worldwide Web provides access to information from the Department of Labor, the Department of Commerce and the International Trade Agency. Datatimes contains a database of business information. Compuserve, Nexis, Delphi and other on-line services can also be mined for valuable information.

GOVERNMENT FILES

Additional information can be obtained from files of local, state and federal governments. Some states require filings under the Uniform Commercial Code when goods are leased or pledged as collateral. One company, curious to know how a competitor could consistently underprice it, consulted UCC filings. It discovered that the rival's depreciation costs were less than half its own. The company obtained from the local building department the name of the manufacturer of the equipment. It found that the rival was using a less expensive brand of equipment in a simpler configuration — and was still getting the job done.

YOUR COMPETITORS

You don't always have to obtain information on competitors through the back door. Often, competitors are willing to share information when they can do so without damaging their own competitive position. Intel, for instance, obtained information from its competitors on their compensation practices. After polling its rivals, the high-tech company shifted from annual to semi-annual employee bonuses. Just be sure you do it the ethical way: by identifying yourself and your company when you ask for the information.

LEARNING FROM YOURSELF

An educated company not only learns from outsiders; it also learns from itself. In a company as diversified as General Electric, it would be easy for one business unit to bottle up the secrets that enable it to achieve quality.

But CEO Jack Welch turned GE into a "boundaryless company," in which knowledge is freely shared. If one business unit develops a piece of technology, the company looks for ways to use it in other units. Thus, GE's aerospace experts helped its medical systems unit to develop an ultrasound technology. When one unit needed help to cope with the expanded demand for gas turbines, it turned to the GE people who knew a lot about turbines: the engineers who designed its aircraft engines.

One good way to spread knowledge around the organization is to transfer personnel across divisional lines. When employees move into new departments, they take with them their innovative ideas. The result is an organization populated by leaders who think about the broad interests of the company and not just the narrow interests of their own departments.

A SEA OF INFORMATION

In this day and age, we're all adrift in a sea of information, but only an educated organization can convert it to knowledge. An organization's personnel may be brimming with technical expertise. But if they have not been equipped through education to seek and absorb the information existing beyond its corporate corridors or plant boundaries, the company will be in a position comparable to that of Samuel Taylor Coleridge's ancient mariner: "Water, water everywhere, not any drop to drink."

Knowledge is the water that nourishes quality in a business organization. In today's information age, it's waiting to be absorbed. But only through education can the people in your organization take it in and use it to put quality into your products and services.

People used to think that quality was expensive. Modern businesses are learning that it's the *lack* of quality that's expensive. Poor quality results in higher costs to correct mistakes and in loss of business as a result of dissatisfied customers. It absorbs workers' time and attention, and cuts into performance and productivity. Quality, therefore, is an important factor in the profitability of your business. An educational system that promotes quality also promotes the Three P's: performance, productivity and profitability.

In Chapter Eight, we'll show how your educational system can provide a pillar in support of other factors leading to the Three P's.

CHAPTER EIGHT

PILLAR SIX: EDUCATING FOR THE THREE P'S

The waning decades of the 20th century filled the air with management buzzwords: Total Quality Management, downsizing, restructuring, re-engineering, learning organizations, time-based competition. You've heard them all.

None of them amounts to a hill of beans until they produce the one thing that keeps business organizations alive and well: profitability.

If profitability is a goal of your company, it should also be a goal of your education and development program. Your human-resource expenditures, like all other expenditures, should yield a healthy return on investment.

Profitability results from a combination of performance and productivity. To achieve profitability, personnel at all levels must know the meaning of these terms and how they can direct their efforts to achieve them. Here are the definitions we use in this chapter:

- *Performance*: The result of effort and resources expended toward executing a company plan.
- *Productivity*: The ratio between input and output.
- *Profitability:* The extent to which total corporate revenue exceeds total corporate expenses.

Let's take them one at a time.

PERFORMANCE

If you are in the manufacturing business, your employees bring their energies and abilities to work in exchange for salaries, wages and commissions. They apply these abilities and the company's other resources to the raw materials to produce a quantity of finished products. If you're in the service industry, your employees use these resources to provide valuable services. In whatever business you're engaged, your salespeople put your resources and theirs to work to seek customers or clients. This is performance. It isn't the same as productivity, and it certainly isn't the same as profitability. But it's where it all begins. Unless your employees are able to deliver peak performance, they won't be able to deliver peak productivity, and your profitability will not be all that it can be.

For performance to be effective, it must be directed toward the achievement of your company's plans and strategies. Your efforts should be guided by your vision and corporate mission, which are based on your corporate values.

Your employees therefore must be fully familiar with the vision, goals and strategies if they are to deliver peak performance. Suppose your strategy calls for marketing your products to a broad spectrum of small businesses. Harry Hotshot, your eager-beaver salesperson, goes out and makes a huge sale to Intercontinental Megaproducts, the global conglomerate. The task of supplying and servicing the giant company monopolizes your company's resources and makes you a *de facto* subsidiary of the client. Harry has put out the effort and brought in the results. But is this the performance you wanted?

Your education and development program should emphasize the company's goals, plans and strategies. Your employees should be thoroughly familiar with the direction in which you want to apply your energies and resources.

Once your employees are familiar with what the company stands for, where it is, and where it is going, you have laid the groundwork for performance. But many other factors affect the level of performance your employees will deliver.

Here are some of them:

- Job matches
- Management styles
- Motivational environment

- Expectations

JOB-MATCHES

You'll go broke if you try to run a limousine service with a fleet of four-wheel-drive utility vehicles, and you'll go just as broke if you try to run African safaris with a fleet of stretch limos. Each vehicle performs superbly in its intended role, but when you try to force it into an incompatible role, performance drops drastically.

People are like that too. We each follow a specific behavior style that is compatible with some roles, less compatible with others.

Some people have natural take-charge personalities. They are outgoing, decisive and competitive. They take the lead and assume that others will follow. They are big-picture people who are impatient with details. They like to project a grand vision and let others work out the details of implementation. They are more comfortable giving orders than they are following instructions. They are long on action, short on tact.

Some people are natural socializers. They have effervescent personalities and tend to put fun into every group and every task. They're good at building enthusiasm in others and involving them in cooperative undertakings. They are miserable when they have to work alone. They love compliments and love to play to audiences. They, too, are oriented toward the big picture rather than the details. They love to try out new things, sometimes implementing them before they're thoroughly tested. They thrive on friendly competition and are devastated by public criticism.

Some people are natural diplomats. They like to be of service to others and they dislike conflict. They are steady, loyal and supportive, and would rather build consensus than give orders. They can work well with others or in isolation. They like to find comfortable routines and follow them. Change upsets them, and instability alarms them. They prize security and serenity.

Still others are natural technicians. They value precision and accuracy in everything they do. They are less concerned with the way they measure up to others' expectations than they are with the way they measure up to their own inner standards. They are cautious, abstaining from action until they are positive all the conditions are right. They believe in doing things correctly or not at all.

Each of us embodies some of the characteristics of all four styles, and all of us can learn to function in any of the styles when circumstances call for it. But each of us has a style that we prefer, and we're happier and more effective with tasks that allow us to work within that style. When we're following our preferred style, we have the wind to our backs. When we're following a contrasting style, we have the wind in our faces.

People following each behavior style are motivated by different things. They learn in different ways and manage people in different ways.

Good leaders know their people and tailor their assignments to the dominant behavior style of each person. They also coach and direct according to the appropriate behavior style. When you have an organization full of people forced to work outside their behavior styles, you have an organization full of stress. This leads to low performance.

When you have managers and supervisors who are unable to relate to the behavior styles of the people they're trying to lead, you have an organization full of resentment and fear. This too leads to low performance.

When you have teams with an inappropriate balance in behavior styles, with action-oriented leaders sounding "charge" and precision-minded technicians crying "wait!" you have an organization full of frustration and dissension.

A knowledge of behavior styles and how you can identify them can be of benefit to people at all levels of your organization. It is especially helpful for those who must manage or supervise others. An education in behavior styles can equip leaders to approach people in the most effective ways, deploy them in the most effective tasks and thus help them achieve top performance.

MANAGEMENT STYLES

Management consultants, myself included, have been preaching the gospel of participative management for a number of years now, and some of the world's most successful companies have been listening.

But participative management isn't something you can spring on people overnight. You can't just walk onto the work floor and say "Starting today, you're all going to become members of self-managed teams."

The degree of employee participation in decision-making must depend on the level of maturity in the work group. Some workers can function as teams with little or no supervision. Others need close supervision. Some teams with a low level of maturity can be educated toward a decision-making capacity. Others may always need some level of supervision.

Maturity, in this sense, means the willingness and ability to set goals, assume responsibility, and perform the tasks necessary to the job.

Supervisory approaches can be divided roughly into two categories:

- Production-oriented
- People-oriented

The production-oriented approach puts more emphasis on the task being performed than on the people who are performing it. Production-oriented supervisors will determine what needs to be done and how it should be done. Then they will tell the employees what to do and how to do it.

People-oriented supervisors will explain the work group's mission and allow the group itself to determine how to fulfill the mission. The supervisors will provide coaching and counseling. They will make sure that the employees have the necessary tools and training, and they will work toward providing a congenial environment. But their roles will be more consultative than directive.

Usually, the people-oriented approach results in higher performance. Studies at the University of Michigan have shown that, as a general rule, light supervision results in higher performance than does closer supervision.

But light supervision will fail in a work group that is not ready for participative management. And some groups, and some tasks, may never lend themselves to complete self-management.

There are advantages and pitfalls to both management styles. Leaders can become so concerned with making their employees happy that they forget what they're there for: to produce an end product or service at a profit. It's possible to have a work force that is so relaxed and happy that it gets nothing done. That's why education is needed to instill in your work force the initiative and self-discipline necessary to function in a self-managed mode. A self-managed team must be able to determine what it needs to do to fulfill its mission. It must have the self-discipline to do what has to be done. It must be familiar with the company's policies and standards and willing to enforce them among its members. These are attitudes acquired through education. When you apply them on top of the skills obtained through first-rate training, you have a winning team.

It's possible to achieve high performance in the short term through rigid and stringent work requirements without regard for employee morale. But in the long term, managers must strike a balance between the two styles.

That's why it's necessary to provide education in management styles for managers and supervisors. Ideally, a group characterized by low maturity should receive close supervision until the level of maturity rises. As the group becomes more mature, the approach can shift gradually from a production to a people orientation. A skillful manager, educated in behavior styles and management styles, knows the work force and knows how to strike the balance.

XEL Communications Inc., a telecommunications equipment manufacturer, has devised a flexible approach to participative management that allows for different levels of maturity. It has devised three levels of work-group leadership:

1. *Supervisors.* XEL supervisors fit the conventional job description. They can assign tasks and discipline employees.

2. *Facilitators.* Their job is to ensure that a team functions smoothly. They have low-level disciplinary authority, but their chief function is to help teams remove obstacles that are impeding their performance.

3. *Schedulers.* These people are first among equals. They take their places on the production lines along with other team members, and are not invested with supervisory responsibility. They are expected to preside at team meetings and represent the team at weekly production meetings. XEL's pay system is based on the skills an employee has mastered, and since scheduling is considered a skill, the scheduler receives extra pay for this skill.

Whether a team gets a supervisor, a facilitator or a scheduler depends on its level of maturity, as determined by the managers. Most teams have schedulers, who are chosen by the team members themselves. Supervisors and facilitators are chosen by managers. Facilitators are usually assigned when teams are having trouble making their numbers. As one team member explained it: "When there's a problem like a parts shortage, you've got somebody that can attend to it right there, and the rest of the team members can keep going. They don't have to come to a screeching halt."[1]

When management assigns a supervisor to a team, it usually means the team is having problems and is making no progress toward solving them. Supervisors and facilitators are expected to work themselves out of their jobs, helping the team solve its problems and to reach a level of maturity that will enable it to become self-managing again.

MOTIVATIONAL ENVIRONMENT

Nobody does anything without motivation. Motivation, quite simply, provides people with *reasons* to act.

A large fruit company thought it was bringing enlightenment and prosperity to a South Pacific island community when it began harvesting fruit there. The natives worked hard and performed well — until they had earned enough money to buy food for their families. Then they would stop work and enjoy life until the food ran out.[2]

The company soon realized that the natives had simple tastes and simple desires, which could be satisfied with a minimum of work. Once they had satisfied their desires, they saw no need to work.

So the fruit company provided the workers' wives with Sears, Roebuck catalogs. Soon the natives were working industriously to buy their families all the luxuries they saw illustrated in the catalog. They now had motivation to work.

Unfortunately, Sears has discontinued its catalog, and anyway, not all motivational problems can be solved so simply.

Surveys across the decades have shown that the top five motivational factors for American workers are:

1. Interesting work.
2. Full appreciation of work done.
3. Feeling of being in on things.
4. Job security.
5. Good wages.

KEEPING THEM INTERESTED AND INVOLVED

Members of the post-baby boom generation, in particular, want jobs that are stimulating, interesting and fun. And they want to feel involved and appreciated. Their expectations run into a hard fact of life: Not all jobs are inherently stimulating, interesting and fun.

But if you're in management, you can look for ways to add spice to humdrum tasks. You can involve employees in group undertakings such as quality circles and task forces. You can encourage employees to upgrade their skills, learning to perform a variety of tasks in team settings. You can keep them informed of the company's goals and its progress toward those goals, so that they feel that they're part of the organization. And you can make sure your managers and supervisors know how to give constructive, upbuilding feedback. A well-timed commendation and a well-chosen reward can do wonders for employee morale.

Some companies hold regular staff parties at the end of the Friday work day, giving employees, managers and supervisors a chance to relax and intermingle over refreshments. Time is set aside to recognize employees for their achievements, and the recognition is usually accompanied by cheers from co-workers.

PROVIDING JOB EQUITY

Good wages rank fifth on the list, which shows that they are important, but not all-important.

The thing to remember is that people look for equity in their jobs as they do in everything else they do. They expect the rewards to be at least as great as the effort. If the rewards and the efforts are significantly out of balance, they look for ways to balance them.

When the reward is disproportionately low compared with the effort, employees may seek to restore balance by reducing their efforts. They may cut back on their performance or they may pay less attention to quality. They may stretch their breaks and lunch hours, or call in sick when they're actually on the golf course. Either way, performance suffers.

If employees perceive that the rewards far outweigh their efforts, they may feel guilty. More often than not, they're able to overcome their guilt and accept the rewards. But sometimes they will overwork themselves to justify their rewards and benefits. This can result in stress, leading to burnout, and — in the long term — lower performance.[3]

EXPECTATIONS

Employees generally live up to — or down to — management's expectations. If you believe your employees are capable, conscientious and trustworthy and let them know you expect them to display those qualities, you'll probably get those qualities.

This is the well-known Pygmalion effect, named after a character in Greek myth who sculpted a woman who was so lifelike that he fell in love with her. The goddess Aphrodite turned her into a real woman, so Pygmalion got a lover who was created in the image of his expectations.

You can create a work force in the image of your expectations. The secret is to set challenging goals for your employees and let them know you believe in their ability to attain these goals. If you set targets that can be attained with minimal effort, minimal effort is what you will get.

A couple of examples will make the point.

LOW EXPECTATIONS, LOW PERFORMANCE

In a California bank, management noted an increase in the number of bad loans, so it reduced the lending authority of its officers. The officers, sensing that management had lost confidence in them, became overly cautious in approving loans. As a result, the bank lost business to its competitors. When it saw what was happening, management reversed itself. The lending officers, yielding to top management's discretion, now went to the other extreme and began making questionable loans. Instead of educating its lending officers in credit evaluation, bank management simply imposed its judgment over theirs. This signaled a lack of confidence in lending officers, and the officers fulfilled the low expectations.

HIGH EXPECTATIONS, HIGH PERFORMANCE

A district manager for an insurance company once demonstrated the value of positive expectations. He organized his sales staff into three teams. He put all his top people into one team under his top manager. He challenged this team to produce a premium volume two-thirds as high as the previous year's total for the entire agency.

He placed his middle performers in a second team and his poorest performers on a third team.

The top team quickly became known as the "Superstaff," and its performance grew significantly, exceeding the manager's expectations.

The middle team increased its performance even more than the Superstaff did. Its manager refused to believe that he and his agents were less capable than the top team. He built up the confidence of his team members and challenged them to outperform the top team. The agents lived up to his expectations.

The bottom team's performance fell off. Knowing that little was expected of them, they produced little. Many of these agents quit the agency for other jobs.

German philosopher Johann Wolfgang von Goethe said it well: "If you treat a man as he is, he will stay as he is. But if you treat him as if he were what he ought to be, he will become that bigger and better man."

COACHING FOR HIGH PERFORMANCE

Of course, expectations alone won't get the job done. Good coaching is needed to help employees stay on track toward the ambitious goals you set for them.

This calls for managers and supervisors educated in the art of articulating the desired performance, recognizing good performance when they see it, and rewarding it in ways that encourage employees to continue it. Your leaders must also be able to help your employees solve the problems they encounter on the way to meeting your expectations.

Leaders must also be able to give tactful, constructive criticism. Criticism can provide motivation to improve or it can be devastating to morale.

Julius Tahija, who went to work for Caltex when it first began oil development in his native Indonesia, drew a dramatic contrast between an effective coach and an ineffective one:

> When I started at Caltex in 1951, I was the most senior Indonesian, handling industrial government and public relations. To be useful, I needed to learn more about oil exploration, so I asked if someone could give me a course in geology, petroleum engineering, and drilling. Caltex put me with a Dutchman the Americans trusted as their expert on Indonesians. He never took the time to train me, and when he ran out of excuses, he was honest: "You know, Julius," he said, "there is an old saying, 'When you know how to make shoes, you ought to stick to making shoes.' Get out of Caltex." I asked for another teacher, this time an American. The difference was dramatic. Teaching me to handle oil rigs seemed to make him happy. As it happened, the work required great strength, and while his huge hands turned the valves easily, I could hardly move them. One day he laughed as I struggled with a valve. "I have the muscle and you have the brains," he said. He never knew how much that meant to me.[4]

PRODUCTIVITY

Productivity, the second element in the "Three P's" formula, is closely related to the first. But whereas performance deals with output — the results of the effort and resources expended — productivity brings input into the equation.

Let's take a fictitious example. Harry Hotshot sold Intercontinental Megaproducts $1,000,000 worth of high-tech products. But to sweeten the deal, he had to promise on-site technical services until the new equipment had gone through a shakedown period. Furthermore, he had to agree to custom modifications to meet the specific needs of International Megaproducts. These modifications required reconfiguration of production lines and retraining of production workers. And the Megaproducts deadline required that Harry's company pay considerable overtime to deliver the products on time.

On the other hand, Prudence Stedfast sold a total of $500,000 worth of products to three different companies that were willing to buy off the shelf. Their orders could be filled without changing the production process or the work schedule, and they required no on-site consultants.

Harry turned in double the performance of Prudence. But when you factor in the cost of filling Harry's order versus the cost of filling Prudence's, you may find that Prudence had the higher productivity by far.

Janet Myers, my bank-consultant colleague, refers to productivity as the ratio between output and input. Many businesses fail to look at both factors when measuring productivity. As a result, they may be getting high performance but low productivity — which translates into anemic profits.

In the service industry, particularly, businesses may overlook the input factor. The costs of providing services are not as easy to quantify as they are in manufacturing, where it's relatively easy to measure the cost of extracting, transporting and processing raw materials. But even in the manufacturing industry, not every manager is aware of the ratio between the total cost of capital and the total value added to a product — which is the final measure of profitability.

The factors affecting productivity can be subtle and intangible; but then, so is depreciation. Yet nobody doubts that depreciation is real and exerts a major influence on the bottom line. If your company has no way of measuring individual or corporate productivity, it needs to develop one. Otherwise, you can't measure your true profitability.

EMPLOYEE MORALE

Employee morale has a profound effect on the productivity of your work force.

In a strictly task-oriented environment, employees with low morale may be coerced into high performance — at least temporarily. Gloomy people can perform mechanical tasks as efficiently as happy people, and machinery doesn't know whether the hands that control it are glad or sad.

But poor morale can lead to absenteeism and high turnover.

Absenteeism hurts productivity in more ways than one. There's the obvious fact that when an employee isn't on the job, the work may not be done, although the fixed costs associated with the work continue.

If the work is done, it may be performed by another employee who is pulling double duty. Or it may be spread among several employees, thereby cutting down on their overall quality and efficiency.

When substitutes are sent in, they frequently are not familiar with the job. The result is low quality and low performance, leading to lower productivity.

Unfamiliar tasks are at the root of a lot of stress problems among business employees. Since stress is behind many of the illnesses and accidents that plague the work place, it also is responsible for driving up health-care costs, thus robbing the company of profits.

Excessive turnover is also a drain on profits. Replacing an employee sometimes costs twice the employee's annual pay.

So the company that invests in high morale is cultivating a stable work force, which in turn reduces the input required to produce its products and services.

Low morale can have a myriad of causes, but they can be grouped into a few broad categories. Here are some of them:

- Underqualified people.
- Bloated organizational structure.
- Understaffing or overstaffing.
- Poor communication.
- An environment of fear.
- Lack of opportunity for advancement.
- Conflict.

UNDERQUALIFIED PEOPLE

Underqualified people at any level are tough on morale. In a team setting, the qualifications are especially important, because an unskilled or incompetent team member affects the whole team's performance.

The most effective place to deal with incompetence is in the hiring process. If your company makes use of self-managed teams, the new employee must be able to adjust quickly to the team culture. That's why it's often advisable to let team members share in the selection process. If they are to choose wisely, they must learn to look for more than technical expertise. They must also learn to probe for the soft skills, such as the ability to deal with conflict.

Few newcomers will be able to merge painlessly into a team setting. Those who have never experienced participative management will encounter a huge culture shock. That's why it's important to have a continuing educational program in place to provide newcomers with the background they need to function in a democratic environment.

Incompetence among managers and supervisors is simply intolerable. While a new member of a work team may affect the morale of a single team, incompetent managers and supervisors spread disgruntlement throughout their spans of control. If a department shows consistently low performance or high absenteeism and turnover, take a close look at your managerial and supervisory people. They may need refresher courses in leadership. Or they may be incapable of making the transition from authoritative to participative management. If they can acquire competence through education, provide the education. It may be cheaper than hiring and educating new managers. If they can't make the adjustment, replace them. Replacing one manager will be much less expensive than constantly replacing team members and putting up with the low productivity and low quality that comes from inexperienced workers.

BLOATED ORGANIZATIONAL STRUCTURE

A cumbersome bureaucracy can be deadly to morale — and to productivity. The management structure at General Motors was a major drag on its competitiveness during the '90s. The giant automaker had grown flaccid during its heyday as the undisputed monarch of the auto world. When Jack Smith took over as CEO in the autumn of 1992, the company had 18 layers of management. Honda and Toyota had only five each.

In such a setting, communication channels become labyrinths and decision-making becomes a nightmare. Nobody knows who's in charge of what function, and efforts to accomplish things get smothered.

No wonder morale suffers.

LACK OF ADVANCEMENT OPPORTUNITY

Nobody wants to work at a dead-end job. Yet many employees, observing wave after wave of downsizing and restructuring, believe that a flattened pyramid means flattened opportunities.

In truth, a thinking organism offers abundant avenues for advancement, but they are different from the avenues traveled by yesterday's upwardly mobile employees.

The traditional reward for good performance in the trenches has been an office and a title. The frequent result was an organization with far more managers than it needed. Fierce global competition has forced the American corporation to trim down to fighting weight, and this has meant the decimation of non-productive middle management and the ascension of knowledge workers, technicians and natural leaders.

If management is to feed the morale of its people, it must find new ways to reward them. It must identify new paths of upward mobility, then make sure its work force knows about them and knows how to get on them.

OVERSTAFFING AND UNDERSTAFFING

The practice of rewarding productive workers by turning them into non-productive managers can lead to staffs saturated with functionaries. When you have more people than you have work for them to do, you create an environment for deadwood. Self-starters will look for things to do. Deadheads will sit around watching the self-starters work. When the go-getters see others slacking off and getting paid for it, resentment results, and morale plunges all around.

When organizations are understaffed, people become overworked. They may stay late on the job or they may take their work home with them. Either way, they suffer the effects of fatigue, and their family relationships are likely to suffer as well. The resultant stress leads not only to plunging morale but also to eventual medical problems.

POOR COMMUNICATION

Poor communication is one of the most common causes of low morale. When your employees don't know where the company is and where it's going, morale suffers. When they don't know whether they're doing well or doing poorly, morale also drops.

Let me illustrate. Suppose you know that there's a treasure awaiting you at the top of a high peak. You start climbing the mountain, but trees and low ridges obscure your view of the summit. You climb steadily until you can barely put one foot in front of another. You wonder how far it is to the top, but you can't tell because your view is blocked. Finally, just as you think you can't take another step, you come to a clearing and the summit is in full view. It may be some distance away or it may be close. But now you know what it's going to take to reach it. You muster the energy and resources and you continue. The visibly diminishing distance between you and your destination provides you with the emotional energy to continue.

The same principle works with your employees. If they can see their objectives and know what it will take to attain them, they will be energized.

Today's employees aren't content with receiving instructions on what to do and how to do it. They want to know about their company and their role in its prosperity. They want to know what products it is producing and how these products are doing in the marketplace. They want to know about the company's long-range vision and its present financial situation. They need to know and understand company policies. They want to know about the benefits it offers and about their chances for advancement.

And they need to know how their own performance stacks up against the company's expectations. If they're doing well, they need to know it. If they need to improve, they want to know how they can improve.

Most companies rely heavily on the grapevine to convey such information. By some estimates, half the information employees receive comes from the grapevine, and in some organizations the figure is as high as 85%. The grapevine is often accurate but seldom complete. It is an inefficient and imprecise way of communicating with employees.

Good communication skills must be acquired at the organizational and the individual level. If the organization can't communicate effectively with its employees, it can't achieve alignment toward a common vision and common goals. If managers and supervisors can't communicate with employees, they can't help them improve their performance and productivity, because good communication is a pre-requisite for good coaching. If team members can't communicate effectively with one another, they can't interact smoothly to get their jobs done.

Organizations and individuals must learn not only to *convey* information and ideas but also to *receive* them. The ability to listen and understand is one of the most important skills in the work place. Healthy organizations provide avenues for employees to communicate with management. And such organizations listen and respond.

AN ENVIRONMENT OF FEAR

Fear often pervades the authoritarian work place. People are afraid of losing their jobs, jeopardizing their advancement, getting chewed out by a supervisor, losing perks and privileges, or getting cut out of the information loop.

These fears dampen the enthusiasm and motivation of employees and can extinguish any creative spark.

Fear in the work place is often the product of management and supervisory behavior. When leaders are abrasive and abusive, their employees come to work in fear. When people aren't sure where they stand with management, they work in a state of uneasiness. Poorly managed personnel systems can create uncertainty and anxiety.

Fear can result when employees are unable to "get to know" the company leadership. Some executives and managers give the impression that they don't want to know their employees. They pass them in the hall without acknowledging their presence. They erect formidable barriers to keep people from finding them in their offices: private stairways and elevators, imposing office doors, a battery of secretaries and receptionists.

Leaders in your organization need to be taught to welcome contact with employees. They must learn to share their successes *and* their failures, their strengths *and* their weaknesses with the people they lead. When employees know that the boss has experienced failure, they're not so afraid of failure themselves. And fear of failure is one of the principal inhibitors of innovation and creativity.

CONFLICT

High morale can't flourish in a work place full of conflict. When people are so busy arguing that they have no time to work, performance suffers, dragging down productivity. Simmering resentment saps energy. It also impedes the interaction among team members, putting the brakes on quality and productivity. When members of a team are competing with one another, their ability to compete in the marketplace is compromised. Sometimes conflict within a team can reach the point that team members are sabotaging one another's efforts. At best, they may hold back information and ideas that might help another team member, and therefore the team effort as a whole.

TAKE THE HOLISTIC APPROACH

Productivity is influenced positively when employees have a holistic rather than a segmented view of the company. Jan Myers produced a perfect example of the way segmented thinking inhibits productivity.

She tells of a bank in which the calling officers (banking's term for salespeople) were going on sales calls without first consulting their Dun & Bradstreet reports, even though such reports could be readily accessed by computer.

The calling officers explained: Each D&B report they called up resulted in a $35 charge to the originating department. The charge showed up in their departmental profit-and-loss statements.

When Jan pointed out that each unproductive call cost the bank $250, they replied: "Yeah, but that doesn't show up on my P&L."

It might not show up on the department's P&L, but it does show up on the company's P&L. The false economy was costing the bank plenty, as Jan Myers knew, because she knew how to measure productivity.

My friend, Joe Jacobs, founder and chairman of Jacobs Engineering, put new vitality into his company when he shifted from a segmented to a holistic approach. During the '80s, Jacobs Engineering's individual offices each operated as separate profit centers. When Joe took on a project that required the pooling of resources from several offices, he found it hard to get the teamwork he needed.

Executives from each office looked at the project from the standpoint of its effect on the profits of their respective offices. Joe solved this by tying each executive's compensation to the performance of the company as a whole. When he did that, he got genuine teamwork — and a jump in productivity. Today, Jacobs Engineering bills almost two billion dollars in fees with shareholder earnings and equity on the rise.

A decade later, First Interstate Bancorp of Los Angeles, the nation's 13th-largest bank holding company, learned the same lesson. First Interstate was a leading commercial lender in 13 Western states. When recession hit the region and borrowers began to default, the bank saw its nonperforming assets (loans on which interest income is not being accrued) grow alarmingly.

CEO Edward Carson took tough measures. He looked at the bank's management structure and realized that each of the 13 state divisions was operating like a separate business, even though federal banking regulations no longer required such segmentation. In 1991, Carson consolidated them into four regions.

Then he replaced the bank's 11 deposit-clearing centers with two large installations. Using advanced technology, First Interstate was able to eliminate redundant administrative functions and cut its 35,000-person work force by more than 25%. The reorganization saved $118 million a year.

The reorganization did more than save money and increase productivity.

Says Lillian R. Gorman, executive vice president for human resources: "For the first time First Interstate was able to see itself as one company with a common strategy."[5]

The principle can be applied throughout any organization. Individuals, teams, departments and business units should be held accountable for the impact they have on total corporate profits and not for the effects on their individual units.

If people are to be held accountable in this fashion, the company must have a well-thought-out strategic plan. People at all levels of the organization must be familiar with the plan, and their efforts must be evaluated according to the way they support the plan. The strategic plan can be your instrument for focusing your organization's performance to achieve peak productivity.

PUTTING TALENT TO ITS HIGHEST AND BEST USE

High productivity demands that you put your talent to its highest and best use.

England's Nuclear Electric found that it could increase productivity by training workers to perform tasks at the next level of responsibility.

By broadening the skills of production workers, the government-owned company was able to relieve its engineers of a great deal of distracting and repetitive work. This increased the productivity of engineers because they could then concentrate on the tasks that called for their specialized training. It increased the productivity of production workers because they could devote their time to performing tasks once performed by higher-paid engineers.

As a general rule, no one in your company should be performing tasks that could be performed by people at a lower pay level.

Executives who rise through the ranks sometimes find this rule hard to follow. The executive who began as a secretary still wants to type her own letters and do her own filing because she believes she can do it better than her own clerical staff. But her time should be spent on the tasks of leadership; the supportive tasks should be performed by her staff.

ENCOURAGE INNOVATIVE THINKING

You can encourage productivity by cultivating in your work force an attitude of irreverence toward "the way things have always been done around here."

Innovation doesn't have to mean high-tech breakthroughs that substitute computers and robots for human workers. It can mean common-sense ideas for reducing the amount of time and effort required to perform a given task.

For example, workers at L.L. Bean, which sells paraphernalia for outdoors people, looked for ways to increase the speed and accuracy of its shipping department. They began looking at their procedures and came up with a simple but effective answer: stocking high-volume items near the packing stations. This saved on the time required to transport the goods to the packing station.

In Utah, the Iomega Corporation looked for ways to cut the production cycle for the computer disk drives it was manufacturing. Part of the solution was grouping its equipment in clusters of related operations. Workers could then assemble the products in one continuous operation. They no longer had to store parts in holding zones for days at a time.

This and other measures helped Iomega cut the production cycle from 28 days to 1 1/2 days — a healthy jump in productivity. The productivity was translated into profitability: The company went from a $36 million net loss to a $14 million profit in five years.

Before employees can produce results such as these, they must cultivate the attitudes that lead to continuous improvements. These attitudes are acquired through education. The role of education can be seen by the experience of Motorola's "ET/VT=1" team. The name is derived from the team's objective: It wanted to ensure that all of the elapsed time (ET) — the time required to handle a requisition — was value time (VT). Value time was defined as time in which an employee was doing something necessary and worthwhile.

Before it undertook the project, the team enrolled in a two-day class at Motorola University. And what did it study?

The "soft stuff": how to set priorities, how to conduct focused meetings, and how to disagree with colleagues without insulting them.

Was the team successful?

Yes. It cut from 67 to 17 the number of days required to handle a requisition. It reduced elapsed time from 30 hours to 3. As a result, purchasing was able to handle 45% more requests without adding workers. That's productivity!

Sometimes innovation may seem to cut into productivity, because performance slows and quality may drop while the new technique is being developed.

One way to minimize this is to set up two tracks — an innovative track and a production track. The innovative track allows people to test new ideas on a small scale before applying them throughout the operation. People should be free to move back and forth from the innovative to the production track.

PROFITABILITY

Performance and productivity, as we have seen, are simply means to an end. The desired end is profitability.

You'd think profitability would be relatively easy to measure. You just subtract your expenses from your revenue.

But how much do corporate leaders know about identifying expenses? And do they know how to measure value added?

Sure, they know how to add up the cost of raw materials, labor, taxes, depreciation and amortization. But how many can tell you the total cost of the capital expended on their individual operations? Sure, they can tell you how much revenue they brought through the door during the year. But how many of them can tell you how much *value* their particular function added to the company's product or services?

"Most corporate groups, divisions and departments have no idea how much capital they tie up or what it costs," observed *Fortune*. "True, the cost of borrowed capital shows up in a company's interest expense. But the cost of equity capital, which the shareholders have contributed, typically appears nowhere in any financial statements — and equity is extraordinarily expensive capital. Until managers figure all this out, they can't know whether they're covering all their costs and adding value to a company."[6]

The after-tax operating profit, minus the total cost of capital, is called "economic value added," or EVA.

When managers learn how to use it, they see their operation in a new perspective. CSX learned, for instance, that it was losing $70 million a year in its intermodal business because of the huge capital represented by its fleet of locomotives, cargo containers and rail cars.

CEO John Snow decreed that the intermodal business had to break even by 1993 or be sold.

One of the first things the intermodal managers noticed was that trailers and containers were sitting in terminals for two weeks between runs. That represented a lot of idle capital. They came up with a way to put the equipment back on the road in five days, allowing them to reduce the number of containers and trailers from 18,000 to 14,000. The company also noticed that crews were using four locomotives to haul freight from New Orleans to Jacksonville at an average speed of 29 miles per hour. The trains were arriving in Jacksonville at midnight — several hours before they were unloaded onto trucks or freighters.

So CSX began using three locomotives instead of four. The average speed was cut to 25 miles per hour, but the cargo still arrived in plenty of time, using 25% less fuel. As a result, the company was able to reduce its locomotive fleet from 150 down to 100, a reduction of $70 million in capital. Intermodal finished 1992 with an EVA of $10 million. What's more, the cost of equity capital dropped: CSX stock soared from $28 a share at the time EVA was introduced to as high as $75 in 1993.

The list of companies using EVA as a measure of profitability includes Coca-Cola, AT&T, Quaker Oats, and Briggs & Stratton, as well as CSX and others.

When your divisional and department heads understand the use of EVA, they can be held accountable for the way the profitability of their units contributes to the profitability of the company as a whole.

But remember: To achieve this overall profitability, you need a work force that is educated from top to bottom in the factors that produce vigorous performance and high productivity.

Profitability, of course, results from quality products or services, efficiently produced, that *sell*. No sales, no revenue, no profit. If you want people to choose your product over a competitor's product, you have to create a *differential advantage* — something that sets it apart from the rest of the field.

The seventh pillar of a good educational system supports the differential advantage. In Chapter Nine, we'll see how to accomplish this.

CHAPTER NINE

PILLAR SEVEN: EXPLOITING YOUR DIFFERENTIAL ADVANTAGE

American poet Ralph Waldo Emerson wrote that "If a man has good corn, or wood, or boards, or pigs to sell, or can make better chairs or knives, crucibles, or church organs, than anybody else, you will find a broad, hard-beaten road to his house, even though it be located deep in the woods."

That may have been true in the 19th century, when Emerson wrote it. Today, you still need good products and services to succeed in business, but being good is no longer enough. Being good gets you into the arena, but it doesn't make you a winner. To win, you need something extra that sets you apart from the competition — that makes potential customers think of you first when they need the products and services you sell. That "something extra" is your *differential advantage* — your DA.

HIGH TECH WITHOUT DA

Recent history is replete with examples of companies that produced good products but got into trouble because they lacked or failed to exploit a DA.

IBM made good mainframe computers, but as this is written, the giant corporation is struggling to return to profitability. It was outflanked and outmerchandised by upstarts such as Apple and Compaq, which rode to success on the personal computer tide.

Compaq, in turn, produced excellent personal computers. In fact, Compaq computers offered more technology than many consumers needed, or were willing to pay for. In time, other companies came out with cheaper versions, and Compaq was forced to restructure and re-orient its product line and marketing strategy.

Intel once had 100% of the market in microprocessors — the brains of IBM-style PCs. Then another company cloned Intel's most powerful chip. Not having to bear the development costs, it was able to undersell Intel, which lost 25% of its market share before it instituted a turnaround.

AUTOMOTIVE DISAPPOINTMENTS

You may be able to think of other good products that didn't succeed, or that flourished for a while and then faded. Chrysler Airflow was an innovative, well-engineered car of the '30s, but it was a sales flop. Ford's Edsel suffered a similar fate in the late '50s and early '60s, not because it was a bad car but because it offered few if any advantages over established makes, including its own corporate cousins.

Another instructive example in the automobile industry is the Rambler, which started life under the Nash nameplate and later stood on its own as the flagship of American Motors Corp. Rambler flourished during the early '50s, when the mass of American motorists was being seduced by the "bigger and better" pitch of the Big Three. Paradoxically, it languished during the '60s, when the compact field, which it pioneered, became a fixture in the American automobile market.

WHY THEY FLOPPED

What explains the poor performance of these good products?

Each failed to achieve maximum acceptance among consumers because it either lacked or failed to exploit a differential advantage.

Your DA may come from doing things faster, cheaper, more skillfully or more thoroughly than any of your competitors. It may come from having more experience, more specific knowledge or more convenient locations. It may come from being the biggest, the most flexible or the most accessible of all the companies in your business.

Or it may consist of the ability to meet the needs of customers in a way no one else can quite match.

IBM: MAINFRAME OUTMODED

In the case of IBM, its DA was its ability to produce and service main-frame computers that were able to handle the needs of large corporate customers. Its DA dwindled and vanished when the competition developed personal computers that could perform the same tasks more cheaply and more flexibly.

TOO MUCH HIGH TECH AT COMPAQ

Compaq's DA was eroded when the competition was able to duplicate its models without sustaining the high cost of product development. The company responded by redirecting its engineering toward high-quality computers at low prices. Its DA was still high technology, but technology that was focused more carefully on the actual needs of customers.

INTEL OUT-INNOVATES

Intel answered its competition by exploiting its DA: the ability to develop more powerful microprocessors faster than the competition could clone them.

EDSEL: NO ROOM FOR ANOTHER BIG CAR

In the case of the Edsel, Ford was attempting to match the differential advantage of its General Motors and Chrysler competition. At GM, the buyer of a low-priced Chevrolet could trade up through the hierarchy to a Pontiac, Oldsmobile, Buick and, eventually, a Cadillac. A Chrysler customer could start with a Plymouth and progress through the Dodge, DeSoto, Chrysler and Imperial lines. But Ford had a gap in its line-up between the medium-priced Mercury and the luxury-priced Lincoln. It tried to plug it with the Edsel, but by that time, the demand for big, gas-hungry medium- and high-priced cars dipped and there was no room for a new entry. Ford later found its differential advantage in its ability to create whole new concepts in automobiles: the four-passenger Thunderbird, the sporty Mustang, the four-wheel-drive Bronco, and the front-wheel-drive Taurus/Sable.

RAMBLER LOST ITS DA

Rambler flourished at first because it offered motorists a DA that the Big Three weren't matching: A compact car that was larger and more powerful than the imports, but not as bulky or as thirsty as full-sized American cars. That differential advantage vanished when the Big Three introduced and heavily promoted their own compacts, which featured more up-to-date engineering.

CUT YOUR EMPLOYEES
IN ON YOUR DA

Whatever field you're in, look for your differential advantage, and make sure your employees know what it is. Fred Friendly built Federal Express by identifying a simple but challenging DA: "Absolutely, Positively, Overnight."

This iron-clad promise of overnight delivery would have landed Fed Ex in the dead-letter file if its employees had not known about its DA and if they were not committed to maintaining it.

If your DA is to be potent and effective, it must involve your employees, from top to bottom. They must know about it, feel that they're a part of it, and support it wholeheartedly. The only way to achieve this kind of buy-in is through an education and development program centered on your DA.

CREATING YOUR DA FROM SCRATCH

Sometimes you have to create your DA from scratch. For example, in the mid-1980s, Bill Sanko and his partners bought out a small, struggling telecommunications equipment company that had once been a part of GTE Corp. and did much of its business with GTE. They gave it an ambitious name: XEL.

Sanko, a former GTE executive, decided that it would be unwise to rely solely on the parent company. So he decided to compete for the business of the Baby Bells and the large industrial companies that had their own telephone systems.

XEL was then a small company with only 180 employees, and this strategy would throw it into competition with much larger companies, including AT&T itself.

Sanko decided that XEL's differential advantage would have to be agility — quick turnaround on orders, quick response to customer needs, all done with high quality at a reasonable cost. But at the time, XEL wasn't quick, and its costs were not very competitive. These were challenges that couldn't be confined to the executive suite.

"We needed everybody in the building thinking and contributing about how we could better satisfy our customers, how we could improve quality, how we could reduce costs," said Sanko.

In other words, he needed a work force that could think for the company and act for the company — and that *wanted* to do that. XEL created a vision: "We will be an organization where each of us is a self-manager."

With the help of a management consultant, the company underwent a culture change, switched from the assembly line to cellular production, and instituted self-managed teams. It soon became a model of self-management. It also became quite profitable.[1]

STRETCH TO ACHIEVE YOUR DA

Note that XEL did not base its DA on its existing resources. It looked at the market it needed to cultivate and asked itself, "What do we need to do to provide better service to our customers?"

Then it redesigned its management and production processes to meet those needs.

XEL's DA was not designed to maintain a comfortable status quo. The status quo would have left it dependent upon the good will of a single major customer — GTE. Sanko chose a DA that would require it to stretch toward higher levels of achievement.

That's what you have to do if you want to establish a differential advantage that sets you apart from the competition. Unless you can keep getting better, in ways that are obvious and beneficial to your customers, you will soon be overtaken by the competition. As Will Rogers put it, "Even if you're on the right track, you'll get run over if you just sit there."

When you determine to stretch beyond your present resources, you immediately challenge your work force to innovate. Innovation requires a work force with a foundation of training in technology, techniques and procedures. But this training must be augmented by education that provides the ability to seek and apply new knowledge.

REINVENTING PROCESSES

As businesses look for newer ways of serving their customers, they are increasingly looking beyond their products and their management structures. They are examining and reinventing the processes through which they produce, market, sell and deliver their products.

What they are discovering, in many cases, is that 20th century businesses took Adam Smith's 18th century principle of the division of labor to extremes. Smith's premise was that you can multiply productivity by dividing production into a number of simple tasks that can be performed sequentially by a series of employees. Henry Ford applied the principle to the automobile production floor, and the assembly line was born. At General Motors, Alfred Sloan applied it to the white-collar office environment, and the modern corporate bureaucracy was born.

The principle worked well in both environments until high technology rendered it obsolete. Managers are now discovering that it's pointless to have one person place an order for supplies, another person accept delivery, another check the invoice against the delivery receipt, and another authorize payment. In a big company, the simple task of filling an order might require the sequential actions of a dozen people, spanning an interval of weeks. With modern computer technology, all these tasks might be performed by one or two people instead of four or five, and in the space of minutes or hours instead of weeks.

Such efficiency is achieved not by modifying existing processes, but by reinventing the processes — abolishing some, merging some, subsuming some into others. This calls for creative thinking on the part of the people now involved in these processes. They know more about how their departments function than do the people two or three steps up the corporate ladder. They know about the snags, the detours, and the short cuts. But if the company is to benefit from this knowledge, it has to encourage its employees to use the knowledge innovatively, to generate creative ideas, and to communicate these ideas to the people who can implement them.

In other words, your company needs to cultivate an innovative mind-set among your employees and provide an environment in which creativity and innovation are encouraged and rewarded. This is a job for your education and development department.

FINDING NEW WAYS TO CREATE VALUE

In creating your differential advantage, you don't have to be confined to the processes within your own organization. In the modern marketplace, you're not creating a product or service; you're creating value for customers.

Traditionally, this value creation has followed a linear course, often called a *value chain*. The old-style cotton mill will serve as an example. The value chain began with the seed company, which developed the desirable strain. The farmer turned the seed into a valuable crop. The crop was harvested and taken to the gin, where the seeds were removed and the fiber was baled. From there it went to the yarn mill, where it was carded and spun into yarn. The greige mill turned it into cloth, and the finishing plant bleached it and applied the appropriate finish. Next a stylist produced a fashion design based on the fabric. The garment plant cut it and sewed it into garments, the department store advertised it and displayed it, and the customer took it home and wore it.

At each stage of the process, value was added to the product. In that traditional system, the process called for performing a specific function at each stage, then handing it on to the next link in the value chain. Cotton picked from the same field and the cloth woven in the same mill might end up in a high-fashion boutique featuring designs by Christian Dior and on a WalMart rack for the budget-conscious customer.

Now businesses are beginning to look at the advantages of creating value not along a chain that links vendor and customer, but in an alliance that involves value-creating partners.

In this way, a company can combine its DA with the DA of another company and thus create a new level of value — and a new differential advantage.

For example, Apple Computer's DA was its ability to design user-friendly products. Sony's DA was its ability to miniaturize components for compact products. The two companies merged their DAs to produce Apple's portable Powerbook computers. Both companies profited from the alliance.

RECONFIGURING THE VALUE CHAIN

Richard Normann and Rafael Ramirez, two Paris-based management experts, have proposed that companies shift their thinking away from "value chains" and think instead about "value constellations."

Writing in Harvard Business Review, they explained:

> *Increasingly, successful companies do not just add value, they reinvent it. Their focus of strategic analysis is not the company, or even the industry, but the value-creating system itself, within which different economic actors — suppliers, business partners, allies, customers — work together to co-produce value. Their key strategic task is the reconfiguration of roles and relationships among this constellation of actors in order to mobilize the creation of value in new forms and by new players. And their underlying strategic goal is to create an ever-improving fit between competencies and customers.[2]*

BAMA PIES CREATES SWEET ALLIANCES

This principle has helped Bama Foods Ltd. of Tulsa, Oklahoma — one of my long-time clients — to move to higher levels of profitability. Bama Foods Ltd. is a sweet goods and snack-food manufacturer. It was doing a prosperous business under its own label, but Mike McKee, its sales and marketing executive, decided to broaden its market.

He knew that some companies were too small to invest in the modern manufacturing facilities Bama could provide. But they had their own differential advantages: recognizable products and brand names, and local distribution systems. He also knew that some large companies would rather buy from Bama than invest in their own manufacturing facilities. A large fast-food chain, for instance, could offer Bama Pies an immediate nationwide market that would require Bama years and millions of dollars to develop independently.

So McKee created alliances that combined his company's DA — a high-quality volume manufacturing capability — with the DAs of both large and small companies. These alliances have resulted in higher profitability for all concerned.

Bama's forward-looking policies did not come about by accident. Its CEO, Paula Marshall-Chapman, set the stage for creative thinking through a quality-oriented educational process, called Bama Institute. My company helped to develop the concept and create the materials. Through Bama Institute, Paula made education and development a top priority, and the result has been a higher level of value creation for her company and for its allies.

INVOLVING CUSTOMERS IN THE CREATION OF VALUE

Some companies have involved customers in the creation of value, and have made this alliance their differential advantage.

Normann and Ramirez cite a notable example: IKEA, a Scandinavian company that has became the world's largest retailer of home furnishings.

IKEA achieved success by developing a totally new system of merchandizing. IKEA markets kits that enable customers to assemble high-quality but low-cost furniture at home.

It sells these through large suburban stores that offer ample parking along with coffee shops, restaurants, even strollers for customers who want to take their small children along, and day-care facilities for those who want to get away from the children while they're shopping.

In 1992, about 96 million people filed through IKEA's global network of 100 stores, providing the company with $4.3 billion in revenue.[3]

STEW LEONARD EDUCATES FOR FUN AND VALUE

In the United States, my friend Stew Leonard has achieved phenomenal success with his dairy store in Connecticut. Stew doesn't just sell dairy products. Like IKEA, he sells a total shopping experience. His products are good, but his store is full of innovative devices that make it fun to go there and shop.

For instance, Stew made his shopping bag world famous by paying customers $3 each for pictures of themselves with the bag — pictures suitable for display on his bulletin board. Stew was rewarded with pictures of people holding his bags while climbing the Great Wall of China, while SCUBA-diving in the Bahamas, and while enjoying themselves in other exotic settings. His customers became his allies in promotion — and they thoroughly enjoyed it.

Stew also involved his customers by setting up a strawberry counter where customers could pick out their own strawberries. He soon found that strawberry sales increased, because customers who came to buy a quart of them would get carried away with the fun of it and would buy two or three quarts.

Stew Leonard is a great believer in education. He institutionalized it at his store through Stew Leonard University which offers customer-service seminars conducted by his daughter, Patty.

YOUR EMPLOYEES CAN HELP YOU FIND YOUR DA

Whatever your business, employees educated for innovation will look for ways to establish and exploit a differential advantage. They will look for things that you can do better than anybody else, and they will find ways to do them better. Or they will look for things you *ought* to be doing better than anyone else and find ways to excel in them.

All it takes is the proper mind-set acquired through education. Here are some examples of differential advantages that have brought prosperity to smaller companies:

A PERMANENT PRESS

Men's Wearhouse of Houston sells name-brand suits, including those by Yves St. Laurent and Dior. So what? You can get those suits at major department stores, too.

Men's Wearhouse, though, developed two differential advantages:

- It sold its suits for 25% less than department stores.
- It promised to press forever any tailored suit that it sold.

A SUPREME COURT OF FOOD

Riser Foods Inc., in Ohio operates a chain of supermarkets, a grocery wholesale business and an ice-cream manufacturing plant. What could it offer to set itself apart from other food stores? Riser recognized that many of its customers were not just interested in buying groceries. Some of them would enjoy eating right there in the store. Others would like to buy food already prepared and take it home to eat. To meet their needs, Riser set up food courts in its markets. It called each court "The Supreme Court." Like IKEA and Stew Leonard's, Riser involved its customers in the creation of value.[4]

HIGH STYLE, LOW PRICES

Bombay Company designs its own furniture products and oversees the manufacturing. My headquarters are in High Point, North Carolina, which means I am surrounded by the largest concentration of furniture manufacturers in the world. What can Bombay offer that differentiates it from these major manufacturers?

Bombay aims its products at people with discriminating taste in furniture but with modest budgets. Such families ordinarily would not be able to afford the furniture they want, but would not be satisfied with the furniture they can afford. So Bombay chose to produce low-priced reproductions of English-style furniture, prints and accessories, designed by Aagje Nourse, its executive vice president. Early on, its most expensive offerings were under $500, and most were under $200.

Bombay chose not to offer its wares in Spartan warehouse-style stores. Instead, it chose upscale retail centers, mostly malls. Ralph Waldo Emerson to the contrary notwithstanding, location does matter. Bombay arranged its furniture displays so that customers could see what the creations would look like in their homes. While retail furniture sales generally were declining, Bombay posted sales gains of better than 22% for five straight years. Its DA made the difference.[5]

UPSCALE DA: MADE-TO-ORDER HEIRLOOMS

At the other end of the price scale, furniture-making entrepreneurs are executing skillful end runs around the large merchandisers by offering customers one-of-a-kind heirlooms.

Sawbridge Studios in Chicago represents 10 craftsmen who build furniture to order. Barry Newstat Furniture in Chicago also custom builds furniture. A small end table might cost $450, while a large chest of drawers might be about $4,000. In Woodstock, Vermont, Charles Shackleton's furniture creations flourished despite prices ranging from $1,700 to $4,500 per piece. New York's Toad Hall also reported rising sales for the 20 cabinetmakers it employed.[6]

Here, craftsmanship and uniqueness form the DA. These craftsmen exploit the demand for products that only people with their skills can produce. They satisfy the needs of customers looking for more than high quality and high style. They aim their products not toward a faceless mass market, but toward people for whom their creations would have personal meaning.

IDENTIFICATION IS THE KEY

This is what I call *identification*, and it is the key to all effective marketing. When people can readily see themselves using and benefiting directly from your products or services, they become interested.

When they can instantly spot the value in it for them, they will believe your marketing claims.

When they see more value in your unique resources than in the resources they are currently using, they will want to know more about them.

When they see that what you can do for them has more value than the money they'll have to invest in it, they will become customers or clients.

The better you can translate your unique DA into specific value to the customer, the stronger will be your marketing appeal.

But before you can sell your clients and customers, you have to sell the people within your company.

That means you have to market internally. You have to sell your own people — even yourself — on investing the necessary resources so you can get the job done and get it done right. That calls for education and development.

Where do you begin in creating your own Education and Development Department?

Chapter Ten points the way.

CHAPTER TEN

EDUCATION THAT DOES IT YOUR WAY

This book began with the advice, "If your organization has a training department, abolish it."

From that point on, we have been building the case for an education and development department to replace your old training department.

By now you may be asking, "Where do I start?"

Establishing a good educational system involves 10 basic steps:

1. Commitment
2. Assessment
3. Conceptualization
4. Structuring

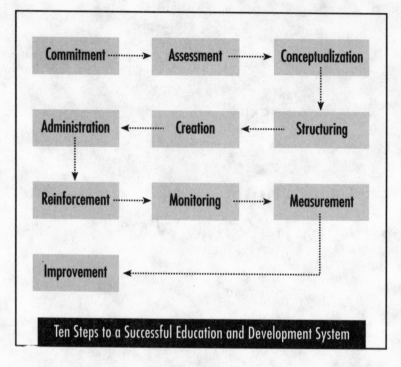

Figure 10-1

5. Creation
6. Administration
7. Reinforcement
8. Monitoring
9. Measurement
10. Improvement

COMMITMENT

A good education and development process requires a solid commitment on the part of top management. When our company designs an educational system for an organization, we start with the top executives. I usually take them on a week-end retreat to get them away from the cares and concerns of the everyday work world. It's important that top management buy into the process, because it needs to send a message to everybody in the company: Management believes in the importance of education.

This commitment is important. A truncated educational process represents wasted money and effort. Yet many top executives put education in the same category as advertising: the first part of the budget that feels the axe during a business downturn. Smart executives know that when business is bad, it's time to advertise. They also know that whether business is good or bad, education must go on.

If the educational process is to succeed, top management must spearhead it. Middle management must be strongly involved, but the CEO should send a firm, clear message: The company is firmly committed to top-to-bottom education and development.

ASSESSMENT

Once you have the commitment, the next step is to assess your needs.

Andrew Forrest, director of human resources for the British Industrial Society, once observed, "the same organizations that refuse to spend 5,000 pounds [$9,000] on a photocopier without a written evaluation of expected benefits will throw themselves into a grand training scheme with no evaluation at all."[1]

So you should have a clear understanding of your educational and development needs and the benefits you expect to gain from redesigning or reinventing your system.

You begin by asking the basic questions in strategic planning:

1. What kind of company are we at present?
2. What kind of company do we want to become?
3. What do we need to do to fill the gap?
4. What kind of employees do we need to accomplish our objectives?

The answer to the last question should guide you in designing a solid and effective education and development department. What qualities must your employees develop to carry your company from its present reality to the future it envisions?

This calls for a needs analysis. Your needs analysis will determine:

1. What your people already know.
2. Where they are strong.
3. What areas need strengthening.
4. What they need to know to accomplish your objectives.

At the end of your assessment process, compile a list of clear, measurable results that you expect to achieve through your education and development department. The results should be quantifiable: an increase in sales, a reduction in quality defects, more on-time deliveries, fewer customer complaints, for instance. Individuals should also identify objectives.

CONCEPTUALIZATION

During the conceptualization process, you develop a strategy for meeting the needs you've identified during the assessment stage.

Look at your present learning curriculum to determine the extent to which it helps employees develop the qualities you're seeking.

DIVIDE THE CURRICULUM

Divide the curriculum into two categories: technical and behavioral.

Technical subjects deal directly with the creation, processing and delivery of your products and services. In a manufacturing process, they may deal with the operation of machinery. In a service process, they might deal with compliance with governmental regulations, the mastery of a software program, or familiarization with company rules, policies, and procedures.

If you're like most companies today, you'll find your technical curriculum in reasonably good shape. Your people must know how to run the machines and manipulate the software, and they must know the appropriate rules, policies and regulations, or you wouldn't be able to stay in business. Therefore, you probably have a training process that is working adequately if not superlatively.

The behavioral curriculum is another matter. In most companies, it ranges from non-existent to barely satisfactory. Only the really progressive companies have pursued and achieved excellence in this category. Yet the behavioral curriculum is what equips your employees to make maximum use of the skills imparted through your technical curriculum.

If your technical curriculum is already meeting its needs, you may find it unnecessary to make major changes in that area. Ask yourself, though, which employees might benefit from technical training in tasks outside their specific job descriptions.

Remember Julius Tahija, the Indonesian referred to in chapter 8, whose job with Caltex involved industrial government and public relations. He looked for training outside his own specialty, and sought on-the-job training in geology, petroleum engineering, and drilling. Do you have white-collar personnel who would benefit from a knowledge of the technical processes they're dealing with? Do you have people who could do their jobs better if they knew more about what happened upstream and downstream from their work stations? Give them the training.

If your technical curriculum is fine but your behavioral curriculum is undeveloped, you'll need to decide how to address your behavioral educational requirements. Will you use in-house instruction, employing present staff? Will you expand your human-resources staff to include more people who are skilled in behavioral instruction? Or will you outsource parts of your process to consultants?

EDUCATION AS A CONTINUUM

Many companies make the mistake of bringing their people together in a classroom, putting them through a specific course and saying, "Go forth: you have been educated."

This won't work. Education is not a one-time event; it is a continuum. It is a process of understanding, of absorbing and of actuating. An effective curriculum will consist of courses that build on one another, flowing in a logical, consistent order. It should be charted over a period of at least three to five years.

STRUCTURING

With your basic approach in mind, your next step is to structure your process. Your structure should be guided by three considerations: *content*, *packaging*, and *delivery*.

CONTENT

The top companies look for content equity in their educational systems. To achieve this, you must plan your content around your company's actual needs. These needs may vary from one group of employees to another. A self-managing team engaged in a manufacturing process will need one type of curriculum; a department comprising teams of knowledge workers will need another type; your top-management team will need yet another type.

While the content may differ for each category of people, the curricula should be complementary. Your courses should be both topically and functionally integrated.

Topical integration means that all individuals who go through the process are educated in all the areas relevant to their jobs. For example, if you want to teach sales people to sell, you also have to teach them to communicate and to relate to others. A topically integrated curriculum will consist of a variety of interrelated topics.

Functional integration means that people in each functional area receive education that enables them to relate their jobs and functions to those in other functional areas.

An organization's culture has many components that relate in different ways to people in different departments and at different levels. But the components have to mesh if the organization is to function smoothly. You can't adopt a curriculum that helps your line employees develop a participative management mind-set while promoting an authoritarian mind-set in your managers and executives. You can't teach your knowledge workers to be creative and your management people to be risk-avoiders.

Many companies go for off-the-shelf programs with generalized content. That's a mistake. No one can design a generic curriculum that will provide just the right fit for your employees. Develop a tailored curriculum that will communicate *your* values, *your* corporate culture and *your* vision.

Levi Strauss achieved content equity in its educational process by designing it around its "Aspirations Statement" — a summary of the corporate values that would guide the behavior of people at all corporate levels.

Look at your values, your vision and your mission statement. Look at your employees, your supervisors and your managers. What qualities do they need to develop to promote your values, carry out your mission and fulfill your vision?

PACKAGING

Not only must the content be tailored to your organization and its aspirations; the packaging must also be distinctively yours.

Educational materials can be delivered in a broad range of packages: oral presentations, workbooks, audiocassettes, videocassettes, audio-visual presentations, interactive software — the list will expand as technology advances.

A good educational process will coordinate a number of these packages. But for these packages to be effective, your employees must be able to identify them as *your* material. The packages must say "This is us."

I've visited workshops and seminars at which the participants sat behind name cards bearing the logo of the company that generated an off-the-shelf training program. There was nothing in the packaging that told them, "This material is designed just for you, with your company and your responsibilities in mind." Your company's name on the name cards and on any literature packages would be a start toward putting your corporate stamp on the curriculum.

Customizing your educational packages is easier than it sounds. I do it each time I create a learning program for a different organization. The core content may be similar from one company to another. I take this core content and add the customizing touches by making specific references and specific applications to the client company.

It's the same principle builders use when they take basic floor plans and customize them to the needs and tastes of specific customers. Automobile manufacturers use it when they use the same basic chassis and the same mechanical components to create different models aimed toward different segments of the market.

DELIVERY

The third component in your educational structure is the delivery. Your delivery system starts with the personnel in your education and development department. You must analyze their strengths and weaknesses and put together a balanced team.

You'll need some people who are good at providing skill-based instruction. They must be technically competent at the tasks your work force has to accomplish. You'll need others who can deliver effective behavioral courses. They must be good educators and facilitators — people who can think on their own and can help others to think. And when it comes to providing instruction for your top-management personnel, you'll need someone with the standing and stature to command the respect of the people in their classes.

Some companies send their training-department personnel to certification programs. They come back certified to teach a generic course designed by some organization for a broad spectrum of businesses. It's far better to have people who are equipped to teach *your* curriculum to *your* people.

That doesn't necessarily mean that you must develop your behavioral courses in-house. The reason most companies don't have a sophisticated behavioral program is that most management people are not educators. They know their companies, their industries and their markets, but they can't be expected to be experts on education. So there's nothing wrong with outsourcing your behavioral curriculum, so long as it is designed for the specific needs of your company.

You may want to outsource some of your instructors, too. Not all of them need to be full-time employees in your education and development department. Some companies with forward-looking educational systems employ a mixture of full-time trainers, line-on-loan trainers, and contract consultants. In most such companies, full-time trainers outnumber other types — in some companies by as much as 12 to 1. But in some, the contract employees outnumber the full-time staff.

Whether they come from inside or outside the company, instructors should be familiar with your corporate culture, your vision, your mission and your values.

Delivery methods can be as varied as technology and the imagination will permit. Figure 10-2 shows the methods being used by the original 19 members of the Benchmarking Forum of the American Society for Training and Development. As you can see, instructor-led sessions far outnumber all other approaches. So although high technology can be useful, you don't have to invest in exotic equipment to have an effective education and development department.

STRUCTURING YOUR CLASSES

How will you structure your classes?

People learn best when they are among the people they work with, applying principles they will use in their everyday activities. This is borne out by

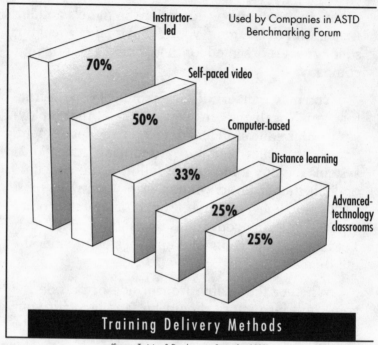

(Source: Training & Development, September 1993)

Figure 10-2

research at the Institute for Research on Learning at Palo Alto, California — funded by the Xerox Corporation as a byproduct of *Nation at Risk*, the report on U.S. education.

The research showed that employees, when dealing with work-place problems, will spontaneously form *communities of practice.*

A paper by IRL researcher Charlotte Linde and others identifies these characteristics of communities of practice:

- The people in them have a shared interest or need to engage in an activity.

- They comprise the people who engage in an activity based on that interest.
- A "mutual practice" occurs when the community engages in its interest.

"We now take very seriously the idea that learning is the process of becoming a member of a community of practice," Linde observed. "The motivation to learn is the motivation to become a member. In communities of practice, people don't just work together. Often they socialize together; in some cases they start to look and talk like each other."[2]

This suggests that the most effective education will bring together people who interact daily in their work lives. Working with a curriculum that addresses the needs of *their* jobs and *their* company, they will be motivated to learn together and to apply together the things they learn.

CREATION

During the structuring stage, you built the skeleton for your education and development process. During the creation stage, you add the flesh and blood and organs.

Manuals must be prepared, video and audio scripts must be produced, visual aids must be readied, and the educational staff must be trained for its new mission.

This is an important part of the process. Your curriculum may be well-rounded and your content may be excellent, but if the tools for delivering them are not well crafted and well coordinated, learning will be impeded.

Most educators agree that people learn best by doing. So effective educators will create tools for involving participants in activities similar to those they will encounter in their jobs.

Classroom lectures must be reinforced by role-playing, problem-solving exercises and simulations of actual work-place situations.

Manuals must be well-organized and easy to use. The writing must be clear, succinct, and geared to the knowledge level and reading level of the people who will be using them.

Video and audio presentations must be well-scripted, professionally staged and technically competent.

ADMINISTRATION

A well-conceived, well-structured process can be derailed by poor administration. Good administration must start with the implementation of the system. Before you put the show on the road, you'll have to choose the staff members who will instruct each course. You'll need to decide on location and timing for the courses. Will they be taught during normal working hours, after hours, or on week-ends? Will they be taught on the work site or off-site?

Your decision will depend upon your individual circumstances. The courses should be timed so that they don't interfere with normal work processes. The location should be quiet, comfortable, and free of distractions.

You may want to test-fly your system before putting it into regular service. A behavioral course, for instance, might be given to a group of management people, who could critique it and pass on suggestions for improving it or eliminating bugs.

If the system is to work, it has to be administered in an orderly, consistent way.

A continuing educational process must follow a well-conceived plan. Who will participate? What courses will they take, and in what order?

A well-structured curriculum will enable you to provide progressive education for your employees as they grow with the company. Individuals can be placed on a specific educational track that equips them not only for the jobs they're doing now but also for the jobs you may need them to do in the future.

Many corporations set up educational programs patterned after colleges and universities. The educational program is tied to an employee's advancement in the corporation.

For example, my company designed an educational system for a regional bank that provided a grid identifying all its employees by job category. We developed a different core curriculum for each job description. Each curriculum contained some required courses and some electives. The grid was color-coded so that employees could see clearly the courses they would be taking.

REINFORCEMENT

The process of understanding, absorbing and actuating does not end when the formal sessions end. It takes time to absorb new attitudes and to actuate new behaviors. So the classroom learning must be reinforced through repetition.

This can be accomplished in a variety of creative ways. Refresher courses can be designed. Audio cassettes containing reinforcing and supplementary material can be mailed to participants. So can written materials. Work-alone exercises can be provided, enabling participants to solve problems at their own pace in the privacy of their own homes.

Don't overlook the value of recognition. Once an employee has completed a course, provide some tangible, visible recognition for the achievement. In the academic world, this recognition is provided through degree programs. How many college students would go through the arduous process of postgraduate study without the knowledge that their efforts would be rewarded with an advanced degree? This same kind of recognition can motivate the employees who participate in your company's educational process.

MONITORING

After your education and development process is under way, you need to ask an important question: Is it working the way it's supposed to?

The most brilliantly conceived instruments may flop when they're exposed to actual classroom situations. Newly designed equipment often develops un-expected bugs; so do newly designed educational processes.

That's why it's important that the human-re-sources department monitor the process. Competent evaluators should audit courses, looking for what works and what doesn't.

The monitoring should cover everything that might have a bearing on effectiveness: Do adjust-ments need to be made in timing and locations? Are the instructors properly matched with the courses? Are they thoroughly familiar with the content and comfortable with the methods of delivery? Is the right kind of equipment available and is it working properly?

These "little things" can make a big difference in the success of your educational system.

MEASUREMENT

During the assessment process, you identified the results you expected to obtain through your edu-cation and development department.

After the system has been implemented, you will need to measure it continuously to determine whether you're getting the results you want.

Your education and development personnel should fully understand the objectives you've set for the process, and their instruction should be aimed toward achieving them.

Results can be measured at four levels:

1. THE PARTICIPANT'S ATTITUDE TOWARD THE INSTRUCTION

This is an assessment based on feedback from participants. One of the most commonly used devices is the evaluation sheet — a form passed out after each course to allow participants to evaluate the content, materials, methods and instructors. These sheets can provide early guidance on whether the course is having the desired effect on participants. Such questionnaires, however, measure immediate and not long-term reactions.

Follow-up interviews, discussion groups, feedback sessions, questionnaires and surveys can provide a more in-depth picture of the course's effectiveness.

One company participating in the ASTD's Benchmarking Forum implemented an automated system for receiving and analyzing participant assessments. It used these assessments to help it with its course-design system, which evaluates course materials before implementation.[3]

2. THE AMOUNT OF LEARNING THAT HAS TAKEN PLACE

This requires before-and-after testing to determine how much additional learning an employee has achieved. The test need not always be your conventional multiple-choice, true/false or essay type questions. Role-playing can also be used. An employee may be asked to perform a job task or to demonstrate a skill before and after the instruction.

The objective at this level, however, is simply to measure the amount of the learning the employee has retained in the short term. It does not measure the long-term application of that learning.

3. ON-THE-JOB APPLICATION OF THE LEARNING

This level also requires before-and-after observations. Questionnaires for employees, their supervisors and their colleagues prior to the course can help establish a base line for an employee's performance. Afterwards, observations from the same sources can help identify any differences in behavior and performance. This level could also involve checking after six months or a year to determine whether the employee is applying the new learning on the job.

Another way of measuring the results of learning is to let employees who have not taken the course serve as a control group, comparing their performance and behavior with those of the group taking the course.

One company uses an informal system for measuring on-the-job application. About two weeks after the course, it will ask participants how it is affecting their work. It collects all written documents from customers, managers, and employees that refer to the results of the instruction. And it asks managers and supervisors what they are observing about the learning results.

4. THE IMPACT ON THE ORGANIZATION

This is where you learn about the dollars-and-cents payback. Look for the quantifiable results you identified during the assessment stage.

In some companies, the instructional staff monitors error rates, calculates dollar figures per error, and uses these data to calculate the net return on their educational efforts.

IMPROVEMENT

Your education and development department should seek continuous improvement as aggressively as the company itself.

The monitoring and measurement are pointless unless you use the things you learn to make adjustments and improvements.

Furthermore, the technology of learning is advancing rapidly. The new information highway will offer exciting new routes to learning. Your HRD should monitor these developments carefully.

Bells and whistles don't necessarily lead to more effective learning. Few companies are entrusting their entire educational processes to methods that eliminate the live instructor. And when it comes to technical training, studies show that there is no substitute for the actual work setting.

But computer-based learning, self-paced video and other high-tech methods can be valuable supplements to instructor-led classroom courses. Evaluate them carefully and use them whenever they offer improvement over traditional methods.

INTANGIBLE BENEFITS

As we have seen, education and development yield measurable results that have positive effects on your company's performance, productivity and profitability.

It yields other dividends that are hard to quantify but easy to spot.

Pride in the company does not show up in a balance sheet, but it can be sensed by an alert CEO who walks the hallways and work areas and interacts with the people.

High morale can't be shown on a thermometer chart, but it is evident in low absenteeism, low turnover, high performance and high productivity.

Good communication, innovation, intelligent risk-taking, and sound decision-making are not as visible as a new piece of capital equipment, but they can contribute even more mightily to corporate prosperity.

The results of an educated work force show up in the work-place environment, in the camaraderie among employees, in the cooperative efforts of employees and management, in the upbeat attitudes of people entering their work stations at the beginning of the day and leaving them when the work day has ended.

In my career as a management consultant, I've formed warm relationships with corporate executives and with human-resources professionals.

It's my hope that this book will convey to top management the message on the lips of so many human-resources people: Today's work force needs training, but it needs much more. It needs a well-rounded education in the behavioral qualities that lead to excellence in every area of corporate activity.

The money you spend educating your people may be the most profitable investment you can make.

Some executives have asked, "What if I spend all this money educating my employees and they leave for another company?"

That's the wrong question.

The real question is, "What if you *don't* educate them, and they *stay*?"

END NOTES

CHAPTER ONE

1. Carroll, Paul B. "The Continuing Crisis at IBM."
    The Wall Street Journal, October 28, 1993, p. A22.

2. Burstein, Daniel. "Future Slot." *The Courier-Journal Magazine,* May 29, 1983.

3. Garvin, David A. "Building a Learning Organization." *Harvard Business Review,* September/October 1993, p. 81.

4. Brown, John Seely. "Letter to the Editor." *Harvard Business Review,* September/October 1993, p. 192.

CHAPTER TWO

1. Henkoff, Ronald. "Companies That Train Best." *Fortune,* March 22, 1993, p. 62.

2. Howard, Robert. "Values Make the Company: An Interview with Robert Haas." *Harvard Business Review,* September/October 1990, p. 142.

3. Quoted from Hewins. *The Japanese Miracle Men.* p. 342. Ruch, p. 42.

4. Bradford, Lawrence J. and Raines, Claire. *Twenty-Something.* New York: MasterMedia Limited, 1992.

CHAPTER THREE

1. Juechter, W. Matthew, "Learning By Doing." *Training & Development,* October 1993, p.29.

2. Sorohan, Erica Gordon. "We Do; Therefore, We Learn." *Training & Development,* October 1993, p.48.

3. Galagan, Patricia A. "The Search for the Poetry of Work." *Training & Development,* October 1993, p.37.

4. King, Pearl H. M. "Task Perception and Inter-Personal Relations in Industrial Training." *Human Relations.* New York: Plenum Pub. Corp., Vol. 1, No. 3, August 1948, pp. 373-392. As cited in *Detecting Training Needs, A Guide for Supervisors and Managers.* Washington: U.S. Civil Service Commission, 1978, pp. 34-35.

5. Frey, Robert "Empowerment or Else." *Harvard Business Review,* September/October 1993, p. 82.

6. Frey, Robert "Empowerment or Else." *Harvard Business Review,* September/October 1993, p. 88.

7. Kelly, Robert and Caplan, Janet "Bell Labs Creates Star Performers." *Harvard Business Review,* July/August 1993, p. 128.

CHAPTER FOUR

1. Hasell, Nick. "Culture Shock." *Management Today,* July 1993, p. 27.

CHAPTER FIVE

1. Frey, Robert, "Empowerment or Else." *Harvard Business Review*, September/October 1993, p. 88.

2. Frey, Robert, "Empowerment or Else." *Harvard Business Review*, September/October 1993, p. 84.

3. Frey, Robert, "Empowerment or Else." *Harvard Business Review*, September/October 1993, p. 84.

4. Frey, Robert, "Empowerment or Else." *Harvard Business Review*, September/October 1993, p. 94.

5. Howard, Robert. "Values Make the Company: An Interview with Robert Haas." *Harvard Business Review*, September/October 1990, p. 138.

6. Frey, Robert, "Empowerment or Else." *Harvard Business Review*, September/October 1993, p. 86, 88.

7. Howard, Robert. "Values Make the Company: An Interview with Robert Haas." *Harvard Business Review*, September/October 1990, p. 138.

8. Maidique, Modesto A. and Zirger, Billie Jo. "The New Product Learning Cycle." *Research Policy*, Vol. 14, No. 6, 1985, p. 299, 309.

9. Brokaw, Leslie and Hartman, Curtis. "Face-to-Face: Managing the Journey." *Inc.*, November 1990, p. 46.

CHAPTER SEVEN

1. Lee, Charles R. "Keep Learning." Letter to the Editor, *Harvard Business Review*, September/October 1993, p. 194, 196.

2. Hillkirk, John. "On Management: Quality down but not out." *USA Today*, November 25, 1993, p. B2.

3. Myers, Janet L. *Productive Bankers and Profitable Banks.* West Lafayette, Indiana: Dearborn Business Group Ltd., 1991, p.161.

4. Garvin, David A. "Building a Learning Organization." *Harvard Business Review*, September/October 1993, p. 86.

CHAPTER EIGHT

1. Case, John. "What the Experts Forgot to Mention." *Inc.*, September 1993, p. 76.

2. Perlson, Michael R. *How to Understand and Influence People and Organizations: Practical Psychology for Goal Achievement.* New York: Amacom, 1982, p. 6.

3. Huseman, Richard C. and Hatfield, John D. "Equity Theory and the Managerial Matrix." *Training & Development Journal*, April 1990, pp. 98-99.

4. Tahija, Julius. "Swapping Business Skills for Oil." *Harvard Business Review*, September/October 1993, p. 72.

5. Richman, Louis S. "When Will the Layoffs End?" *Fortune*, September 20, 1993, p. 56.

6. Tully, Shawn "The Real Key to Creating Wealth" *Fortune*, September 20, 1993, p. 38.

CHAPTER NINE

1. Case, John. "What the Experts Forgot to Mention." *Inc.*, September 1993, p. 66.

2. Normann, Richard and Ramirez, Rafael. "From Value Chain to Value Constellation: Designing Interactive Strategy." *Harvard Business Review*, July/August 1993, p. 55-66.

3. Normann, Richard and Ramirez, Rafael. "From Value Chain to Value Constellation: Designing Interactive Strategy." *Harvard Business Review*, July/August 1993, pp. 66-68.

4. Stern, Gabriella. "To Outpace Rivals, More Firms Step Up Spending on New-Product Development." *The Wall Street Journal*, October 28, 1992, p. B1, B13.

5. Stern, Gabriella. "To Outpace Rivals, More Firms Step Up Spending on New-Product Development." *The Wall Street Journal*, October 28, 1992, p. B1, B13.

6. "Business Bulletin." *The Wall Street Journal*, October 28, 1993, p. A1.

CHAPTER TEN

1. van de Vliet, Anita. "Assess for Success." *Management Today*, July 1993, p. 60.

2. Galagan, Patricia A. "The Search for the Poetry of Work." *Training & Development*, October 1993, p. 35.

3. Kimmerling, George. *Training & Development*, September 1993, p. 29.